...ace Library · DUE DATE (stamp...nally
RETURN D

c.2

DATE DUE			

LIBRARY
EISENHOWER COLLEGE

Second Edition

Acting Professionally

RAW FACTS
ABOUT CAREERS
IN ACTING

Robert Cohen
University of California, Irvine

BARNES & NOBLE BOOKS

A DIVISION OF HARPER & ROW, PUBLISHERS

New York, Hagerstown, San Francisco, London

Originally published by Mayfield Publishing Company, this book is here reprinted by arrangement.

ACTING PROFESSIONALLY. Copyright © 1972, 1975 by Robert Cohen. All rights reserved. Printed in the United States of America. No part of this book may be used or reproduced in any manner without written permission except in the case of brief quotations embodied in critical articles and reviews. For information address Mayfield Publishing Company, 285 Hamilton Avenue, Palo Alto, California 94301. Published simultaneously in Canada by Fitzhenry & Whiteside Limited, Toronto.

First BARNES & NOBLE BOOKS edition published 1977

ISBN: 0-06-463453-1

78 79 80 81 5 4 3 2

PN
2055
C57
1977
C. 2

TO:

Pam	Charlie	Robin
Steve	Annie	Marcy
Bruce	Marc	Jeri
Bill	Dena	Jerry
Denise	Judy	Doug
Jeff	Astrid	Betty
Donna	Elaine	Penny
Eve	Michelle	Mark
Susie	Don	Sidney
Cathy	Jack	Tom
Jim	Richard	Margaret
Larry	Jon	Toni
Mike	Katie	Bill
Wayne	Bob	David
John	Linda	Oakley
	Ernie	

and all that have followed

Contents

Foreword by Richard Quine   ix

Preface to the second edition   xi

° ONE °

Introduction   1
    The industry of the industries   2
    The economics of the acting profession   5
    The art of the acting profession   9
    Maturity in acting   10

° TWO °

What you will need   12
    Talent   13
    Personality   17
    Physical characteristics   21
    Training and experience   25
    Contacts   34

Commitment and will to succeed   38

Attitude and capacity
      for psychological adjustment   40

Freedom from entanglements
      and inhibitions   43

Good information and advice   45

Luck   47

° THREE °

What do you do now?   **49**

Your medium   49

Your home base   51

The LORT–CORST–COST–ADTI–MTA circuits:
      regional theatre   51

Auditioning for regional theatres   53

Unified auditions   55

New York and Hollywood   57

Jumping media   58

Establishing yourself   60

A dependable source of income   60

A telephone and telephone service   61

Photographs   62

Résumés   69

Agents and agencies   71

Getting an agent   75

Interviewing an agent   79

Rounds   82

Getting known:
      advertisements for yourself   85

Interviews   86

Auditions   89

Prepared scenes versus cold readings   95

The screen test   97

The job offer 98

Unions 100

How much will you make? 102

° FOUR °

Other opportunities **108**

Outside the industry 108

Educational theatre 110

Doing your own thing on stage 112

Afterword **115**

Appendix **118**

Published information 118

Books 119

Lists of franchised agents
and producers 120

Lists of summer theatres 121

Lists of regional repertory theatres 121

Lists of dinner theatres,
outdoor theatres 123

Schools of theatre and acting 123

Where to live and eat in
New York and Los Angeles 125

Sample résumé 126

Sample letter 127

TVQ ratings 128

Foreword

Robert Cohen has done the theatrical profession a great service in writing this long-needed book which you are about to read. It is not only an extremely practical guide for aspiring actors and actresses, but a blessing undisguised for show business professionals. Ever since the first star was born, impresarios, actors, producers, directors, casting directors, agents, press agents, and drama coaches have been bombarded by career questions fired at them by young actors. Now at last those beleaguered elders can smile reassuringly and answer almost any such question with an authoritative and explicit, "Read *Acting Professionally* by Robert Cohen."

Having spent nearly my entire life in this fascinating and frustrating profession—performing in vaudeville, on Broadway, in radio, television and motion pictures, and then for many years as a film director, I can only wish this book had been available when I was a fledgling actor. However, thank the Muses, here it is now: a comprehensive guide for the bedeviled by a man who has obviously been through the fire.

To those of you who read *Acting Professionally* and feel only a sense of panic, be grateful. Mr. Cohen has probably saved you from a life of chasing rainbows—an extremely unfulfilling occupation.

To those of you who still choose to dedicate yourselves to an acting career, good luck. You may never see your name in lights but neither does a stonemason who beams with pride at the smoke curling from the fireplace he has built nor a chef who peeks from his kitchen and smiles contentedly at the diners savoring his creations—to wit, the wise men who work at what they love not only for glory but also soul satisfaction.

So read on, ladies and gentlemen. If act you must, learn to act professionally—forewarned and forearmed, unlike actors past, who had not this map to guide them.

Richard Quine

Richard Quine *is eminently qualified to comment on "acting professionally": child star in vaudeville, leading man on the Broadway stage and on radio, Hollywood actor, director of films such as* My Sister Eileen, The World of Suzie Wong, Synanon, Hotel, Bell, Book and Candle, *and* W, *and TV producer and director including various* Columbo *episodes.*

Preface

This book has undergone quite a bit more revision than I anticipated when I first sat down to prepare a new edition. For one thing, the "raw facts" of the first edition, particularly as regards the New York and Hollywood acting markets, have become considerably rawer. Whereas in the first edition I was able to note that only one out of three Screen Actors Guild members grossed an income as high as $3500 a year, the figure now is one in *five*—this at a time when $3500 buys a lot less than it did in 1972. While the profits of the film, television, and Broadway theatre industries have finally begun to rise, this has not translated into greater incomes or opportunities for actors, owing to increased reruns, increased emphasis on fewer and fewer "blockbuster" films, and increased importation of British stage shows. Commercialism has if anything become more cynical and more pervasive, particularly in Hollywood; the "TVQ" personality rating system, for example, uses the opinions of six-year-olds to reverse the casting decisions of directors and producers, and the purveyors of this system are trying to market it in legitimate stage circles. None of this is terribly pretty.

On the other hand, the regional theatre, which had seemed rather dormant after its first great growth in the early sixties, is on the march again. Partly funded by a rapidly increasing National Endowment for the Arts ($75 million in 1975, up 2500 percent from its inception a few years ago), and partly because of increased offerings and new concepts, nonprofit LORT theatres, experimental community theatres, outdoor theatres, and particularly dinner theatres have been doubling and re-doubling their productivity and their proffered opportunities for professional acting careers. Consequently much of the revision has consisted of enlarging the discussions of these areas.

I am particularly grateful in the current revision for the assistance of several of my former students, mentioned in the dedication of this volume, who have written to me of their personal experiences as they fight the battles of their industries themselves. In particular I wish to acknowledge the bright eloquence of Bruce Bouchard, Richard O'Connell, Jeff Greenberg, Jerry Hoffman, and Larry Lott, most of whom I have quoted herein, and the aid of many, many others who have also shared with me their experiences and helped to provide a continuing background of information. I would also like to express my appreciation to Boland Wilson, of Universal Studios, to Buck Harris and Paul Sargent Clark, of the Screen Actors Guild, to Dan Hogan, of Actors' Equity Association, to Mary Ellen White, of the M.E.W. agency of New York and Hollywood, to Marvin Poons of the American Dinner Theatre Institute, to David Frank and Davey Marlin-Jones of the Loretto-Hilton Repertory Theatre, to Duncan Ross, of the Seattle Repertory Theatre, to Jerry Turner, of the Oregon Shakespeare Festival, to Keith Fowler, of the Virginia Museum Theatre, to Frederic Vogel, of the Foundation for the Extension and Development of the American Professional Theatre, and to Mark Sumner, of the Institute of Outdoor Drama, all of whom provided material and assistance in response to my queries; and to Peter Zeisler and Rosemarie Tichler, who invited me to observe the TCG Chicago auditions in 1974. My gratitude also extends to Dick and Judy Bare, the editors of the first edition of this work, and Lans Hays, the editor of this edition—as well as to Lionel Gambill, whose copy editing saved me from some rhetorical excesses, and to Lorna Cohen, whose careful and perceptive criticism proved as stimulating as it was demanding. Finally I must give to the actors—the total list of whom my acknowledgment is only the barest fragment—my respect, my admiration, and my bewildered affection.

Robert Cohen

ONE

Introduction

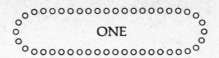

This book seeks to give practical information and advice to people who are considering professional acting as a lifetime career. It is odd to think that thousands of aspiring actors graduate each year from drama schools, colleges, and theatrical institutes, well versed in Shakespeare and Stanislavski, yet almost totally ignorant of the realities of the acting marketplace. It is surely no exaggeration to say that no other profession is so completely misunderstood by the young people planning to enter it.

The reason for the misunderstanding is clear. We are bombarded with misinformation about the actor's life. On the one hand we are continually exposed to the actor-as-celebrity—living out a neo-adolescent fantasy life of Beverly Hills swimming parties, Fifth Avenue penthouses, triumphant tours to London and Tokyo, location shooting in tropical paradises, fan clubs and fan magazines, fame and notoriety.

We are also shown a complementary picture: the actor-as-artist, whose genius is compared to that of Bernhardt, Chaplin, Duse, or Olivier, and whose creative works are the object of study in newsmagazine cover stories. Naturally there is truth in all of these picturizations, but it is only a part of the truth, the part that draws, each year, thousands of young people away from the commonplace goals of motherhood, bookkeeping, and carpentry, and into an attempt to get onto the stage, screen, or tube in any way possible.

Almost all will fail. With the fewest exceptions, these young people, led by fantasies and blinded by ignorance, blunder into the most bitterly competitive marketplace known to man, where they are tossed about mercilessly, like sparrows in a hurricane. It is a needless, pathetic experience, and the fact that it is well enough known to have become a cliché of American soap operas does not prevent its annual repetition.

In this book I examine the contemporary professional situations in which actors are likely to find employment, an examination in which I attempt to ferret out as much of the whole truth as may be found. I am not myself a professional actor; I have no personal axe to grind, no bitterness to mask, and no particular elation to confide. Yet for the past 20 years I have been living, writing, and working side by side with people actively involved in all phases of the professional theatre and film industries—in New York, in Los Angeles, and in the regional theatre circuits. I do have one desire, shared, I think, by nearly everyone in the industries, and that is to describe acting as a profession without promoting it as such. If I can discourage 90 percent of my readers from attempting a theatrical or film career, I will have done some service, because more than that number would fail in any case; and the "discouragable" ones would have been the first to fail.

On the other hand, for those talented, dedicated, and brave souls who are willing and able to commit themselves to an acting career, and who will commit themselves regardless of the hardships and contention they might find, I have tried to collect some useful information and suggestions. Suggestions, of course, are not rules. There are simply no rules for success in the theatre, and there is no proven path to a successful career in acting, much less to stardom. If there were, this book would be unnecessary. There are only decisions to be made and possibilities to be seized, and this book is intended to help you do both wisely and effectively.

The industry of the industries

Whatever else acting might be, it happens to be a job title within some of the biggest industries in the American and international corporate structures. The Broadway theatre and its associated "road" companies generate about $100 million annually. The film *The Godfather* earned rentals of $285 million in its first four years. The *profits* of the American television broadcasting industry in 1973 were $653 million, and the gross income of that business was $3.46 *billion.* These are not the types of businesses that go around the neighborhood to borrow props.

The independence of the acting industries from the rest of the business world, which was somewhat protected by the peculiarities of the dynamic czars of years ago, has become more and more a thing of the past. Most film studios are now wholly owned subsidiaries of international conglomerates—companies like Gulf and Western (which makes metals, chemicals, and Paramount Pictures), Kenney (which owns parking lots, mortuaries, and Warner Brothers), and Transamerica (insurance, real estate, and United Artists). Broadcasting companies have branched into sports (The New York Yankees) and Broadway production (*Hair*), and Broadway producers are funding productions with Hollywood investments. The companies and conglomerates clearly include men of artistic talent and vision, and also men whose interest in the acting arts is directed at its one measurable product: "the gross."

And the "grossers" have the upper hand. "Amazing Grace Grosses!" screams a headline in *Variety*, explaining that the film *Amazing Grace* had an "amazing gross" of $25,206 in its opening week in Memphis. More than a few young actors have wondered if they hadn't picked up the wrong newspaper when they took their first look at *Variety*, the show business weekly (and in Hollywood a daily), which is the bible of the industry. "Grosses" are the prime news on every page.

Grossness pervades the business end of the acting industries. In *Final Cut*,* writer–director Paul Sylbert details his experiences in making the film *The Steagle*, and shows how he was pressured to cast the mistress of an Avco Corporation executive (Avco, of course, owns Embassy Pictures) in a featured part. Lying, stealing, and the perpetually accompanying lawsuits are a well-known feature of the film trade, as described with admirable candor and wit in William Bayer's excellent *Breaking Through, Selling Out, Dropping Dead.* † Even the purest are not invulnerable; the highly publicized invitation of John Wayne to

* New York: Seabury Press, 1974.
† New York: Macmillan, 1971

receive a "worst actor" award from The Harvard *Lampoon* was actually a publicity stunt worked out between "Max Bercutt at Warners, who orchestrated," and the Harvard staffers who gave the "not-so-spontaneous challenge." "One of the biggest media breaks for a film biz publicity stunt in recent memory of trade toutmasters," said the *Variety* reporter who gleefully wrote this story describing the concerted effort between Harvard (Harvard!) and the toutmasters.

While actors play a part in this industry, it is only a small part as far as the money is concerned. Out of the $3.46 billion in gross revenues received by the television broadcasting industry in 1973, Screen Actors' Guild (SAG) members received only about $135 million, or *less than 4 percent of the total.* More than half of this came from "non-acting" appearances in television commercials. Since all filmed television production (including prime-time series, filmed commercials, movies for television—virtually everything except soap operas, newscasts, and game shows) is produced under SAG auspices and under SAG contracts, this is a fairly good picture of how the "gross" pie is sliced. In a book entitled *The Movie Business: American Film Industry Practice,** only 1 chapter out of 34 (consisting of 4 pages out of the total of 370) is in any way concerned with actors (the chapter is entitled "Actors as Union Men"). The section on "Creative Functions" has five chapters: they are called "The Producer," "The Director," "The Team Producer," "The Writer/Producer," and "The Low Budget Producer." Clearly the film or T.V. actor is not the celebrity in his industry that he is in the fan magazines. In live theatre industries, the actor when he gets work is closer to the center of power, but with Actor's Equity Association unemployment hovering around 92 percent (that's right, *un*employment) that centrality is, as a general rule, only academic.

What is life like in and around these industries? A young and talented actor whose career has been marked with extraordinary success in its early stages—with initial employment in the first three months, and continual employment for two years thereafter—a young man never to my knowledge needful of profane language to express his bountiful mind—wrote from New York recently: "It's a difficult mother------g business. It's a p--s. It's for mad people. I mean absolutely insane lunatics have to want to go into this business. There's no secur-

* William Bluem and Jason Squire, eds. (New York: Hastings House, 1972).

ity, hell, there's no security for anyone. And in a business when the work is the only reality you've got and there's no work, it's tough. It can beat the hell out of you." And this seems to be a general, not an exceptional reaction, one that simply cannot be ignored.

The economics of the acting profession

Young people have, as a matter of course, either of two economic goals in mind when they begin to think of acting professionally.

The first goal is the "adolescent" one. They wish to be movie stars and make piles and piles of money.

The second is the "mature, realistic" one. They scorn the piles of money and opt instead for a steady acting job with artistic respectability. They disdain Hollywood and perhaps New York as well, and aim instead for regular employment with a modest repertory company and a reasonable salary—"just enough to live on."

And so it would be—if they could get it.

The tragedy of this situation is that *both* goals are in the realm of fantasy. Too often the actor who "rejects" Hollywood before it has rejected him thinks that by dint of that rejection he has made himself eligible for regular repertory work somewhere else. It is as if rejecting an unoffered Cadillac somehow entitled us to a Volkswagen. The fact of the matter is that the supply of actors so overwhelmingly exceeds the demand that an actor must be one in a hundred to get *any* acting job. One in a hundred, *literally*.

The idea that there are hundreds of paid acting positions in America's regional theatres, and that these are, as a matter of routine, available to professionally inexperienced young actors is a popular undergraduate rumor with absolutely no foundation. A little research shows that it may be easier for some people to get a job in a TV series than a job with a repertory company in Indiana. Employment in *any* of the acting industries is simply very, very, very difficult to get; a young actor with superb college drama credentials should no more expect to get a paid acting job than a political science graduate should expect to become a United States senator.

The fact is that there are frighteningly few professional jobs of any kind available anywhere in the American acting industries. To presume that you might get one of them because you do not ask for very much money is frankly unrealistic. In the first place, almost every one of your competitors (and there will be thousands and thousands of them) are just as hungry for work as you are; and in the second, the unions will keep you from working at less than a minimum wage even if you want to. Since so many are willing to work *at* minimum, your economic bargaining power as a beginner is nonexistent, and your offer to work at scab rates, should you be foolish enough to make it, will be rejected out of hand. Then you will learn another lesson—there's not that much money in acting anyway!

How much do actors really make? There are 30,000 members of the Screen Actors Guild, which is the most aggressive and well run of the acting unions (about which more later). Of these 30,000 SAG actors, less than 18 percent earned as much as $3500 in 1974. That was their *gross* earnings; when taxes, agents' commissions (10 percent), and the expenses of commuting to (and dressing for) auditions and interviews are deducted, we find that in 1974 *less than one out of five working, professional, SAG-unionized actors took home as much as $200 a month.* In New York or Los Angeles, $200 is hardly enough to pay for the rent and utilities for a substandard one-bedroom apartment; still three out of four SAG actors made less, or nothing. The situation for unionized stage actors, operating under Actor's Equity Association (AEA—but more commonly called "Equity") contracts, was even worse. Of the 19,000-odd members in 1972, only a handful more than 4000, or about one in five, made a gross income of as much as $2500 from all legitimate theatre activities. Fully 79 percent made less, and only 888, or less than 5 percent, grossed the standard middle-class income of $10,000 a year. With a general unemployment rate of 80 percent and frequent peaks up to 92 percent at any given time, and the "textbook" for off-Broadway producers (and by implication most non-Broadway producers) explaining that "Almost always the cast is hired for the equity minimum, and their greater remuneration comes from the opportunity to work,"* it is clear that few but starring performers accumulate anything resembling the income of gardeners, plumbers, or schoolteachers. And when the ten-week run ends, and the

* Donald Farber, *From Option to Opening* (New York: DBS Publications, 1968), p. 99.

actor is back on the street for another indefinite period of hunting for work, not much of that minimum has gone into a cushion.

Of course, there is more money in Hollywood than in New York, and in general the figures there when you first see them seem gigantic. The scale for filmed television performing is $172.50 per *day*, and a week's work brings $604. Who could not live, and live well, by getting $172.50 every now and then?

The problem is the every now and then. It involves an implicit multiplication that says, "All I have to do is work only five or ten days a month and . . . ." But we are already into the area of fantasy, because *nobody* starts out working regularly five or ten days a month, supposing that they start out working at all. You may start out with three days in January, two more in March, a day in November, and another two in December, and you will still not clear $1000 after taxes and commissions, and *it's been a great year*. Residuals will eventually add to that, but even including them and doubling everything for good measure, you would have made more on welfare. That is why four out of five Hollywood actors can't make $3500 a year.

We hear, of course, that the theatre and film industries are in a current state of economic depression, and that some new development —financial or technological—will create a golden age for actors in days ahead. This has been said regularly for the past half-century. The Broadway theatre has been called a "fabulous invalid" since the early thirties, and the film industry has suffered a mammoth decline in production since World War II. (There were 763 films released in 1936, 425 in 1946, 232 in 1970, and only 156 in the "great rebound" year of 1974. During that year, despite the fact that U.S. box office revenues grossed close to $1.9 billion—an all time high—only 124 new feature films were released—an all time industry low.) Television, which is regularly held accountable for the virtual demise of the other acting media, has failed to pick up the slack, and is currently in its own decline—as far as actors are concerned. While 39-week seasons and 28-hour prime-time weeks were standard during television's infancy, reruns and regulations have cut and squeezed this to 17- and 13-week seasons, and 25-hour prime-time weeks.* Fully half of prime-time

* Both are likely to change because of the efforts of SAG, which negotiated a contract for 1974–77 that will eventually give actors 100 percent of their original

television today consists of reruns. The great growth of television's broadcasting of sports events, game shows, and old movies has also cut into the opportunities for actors; the sum total of these cutbacks and infiltrations cost actors 16,000 jobs in 1973, and $53 million in paychecks. The situation is hardly better in the industries' allied non-acting positions; 1973 unemployment among Hollywood stage-hands (grips) ran between 30 percent and 90 percent; makeup artists from 32 percent to 67 percent; and cowboy extras a steady 80 percent. These conditions continue to prevail, and many union branches are opening special offices for emergency aid and "career adjustment" assistance. In the final official words of Buck Harris, retiring after a long career as the public relations director of SAG, "Nothing is being done about the fact the whole industry is collapsing here."*

And still they come. For every union actor pounding the pavements of New York, or spinning his wheels in Hollywood, there is a shadow in the wings: a non-union actor (or actors) badgering friends for information, help, a foot in the door, a contact, a job. There are over a thousand colleges and universities offering courses in drama today, and 330 with full-time drama departments that graduate students ambitious to act professionally. Additionally there are conservatories, professional schools, institutes of theatre, community theatres, and eager high school teachers, all of whom tend to point students in that same direction. Finally there are housewives, executives, models, television announcers, sports figures, teenage girls in shops, busboys, ex-mayors, surf bums, and ski bums who are right now pondering the possibilities of making it into Movieland or the Great White Way. These people are the competition of every actor in the business. They are also your competition. They include thousands who are, let's face it, talented, hardworking, dedicated, and backed by glowing reviews from the Denver *Post*, the New Haven *Register*, and the Fresno *Bee*. They all have the same idea you have—to develop a successful acting career—

---

salary (subject to a ceiling) for each rerun—hopefully reducing the profitability of this job-killing device. And SAG is also in negotiation with the Federal Communications Commission to relax its prime-time access rule, which limits network production to the detriment of dramatic broadcasting. Prime time had earlier (1972) been reduced to 21 hours. Some of the difference has subsequently been restored.

* Los Angeles *Times*, February 19, 1973.

and some of them may even be more cutthroat and determined than you!

The art of the acting profession

It is clear that most actors live at a standard severely below the established poverty level. Furthermore, lack of money creates enormous problems for people who not only have to live, eat, and stay healthy, but must dress well, look well, buy photographs, and drive around to auditions. Still, the financial deprivation is one that most actors are willing to put up with—at least for a while—because they are pursuing something far more important than money. They are pursuing their "art." Sadly, however, the industry will almost certainly disappoint their "mature" artistic hopes as well as their "adolescent" yen for fame and riches.

A well-known film producer used to send his cast and crew a telegram on the first day of shooting for each picture. The message was "Forget art, make money." "Forget" was not the word he wanted, but it was one that Western Union would send over their lines. Most producers live by this message, and a huge amount of purely commercial claptrap is marketed both in Hollywood and New York, and even by the resident regional theatres, some of whose producers actually brag about it. In the words of one midwestern theatrical producer/director: "I am not in the theatre business, darling, I am in the ass business. I am in the business of putting asses in my seats."

A review of the film *The Love Machine* in *Variety* made this significant point: "The secret of a film like this, rarely spoken outside of inner sanctums, is that if it were better written, better directed, and better acted, it would probably fail." The industry's prime goal is to make money and your value to the industry is determined precisely by how much money you can make for it. Art is a secondary consideration in most industry enterprises, and no "new wave" or "new theatre" has made a lasting dent in this principle.

Certainly there are many people in both Hollywood and New York who make money and art at the same time, but there are also many who make money without making art, and who are only too happy to admit it. Here is the schizophrenia of show business. It is both commerce and creativity, and the two are almost invariably in conflict. With every act of genuine creation, there is a follow-up of massive, noncreative exploitation. Originality, which is the hallmark of the artist, is an invitation to financial disaster; and those who call the tune—angels, sponsors, and corporate producers—are all too eager to copy last year's success rather than experiment with an untried commodity. When the price of a big Broadway show runs close to a million dollars, and of a film up to twenty million, the producers will tend to imitate whatever previously successful models they can find. Thus are the new genres created: the "homesteading" TV series, the "folk Jewish" musicals, and the sexploitation films. Successful plays, movies, and television shows replicate like cancer cells, and films, for example, that are advertised as "this year's *Godfather*" (or worse, "this year's *Godfather II*") dominate an industry that often cannot tolerate truly artistic creation.

There is a common impression in the business that, for acting, New York is a more artistic milieu than Hollywood, and regional repertory more artistic than New York. Like all generalizations, however, this can be counted as only partly correct. There are artists in Hollywood and on the other hand, there is vice, graft, exploitation, indolence, and greed throughout *every* phase of the theatre. In general, you are going to have to tread carefully between art and money, and you will have to hang on to your integrity with an iron grip.

Maturity in acting

And you are going to have to be mature. What does that mean? It means to accept and work within the basic structure of adult society. Difficult for everybody, this is particularly difficult for the actor, whose "art" demands from him everything that is childlike, sensitive, vulnerable, and even innocent. How to maintain these qualities in a world that is directed at the gross, that runs on guidelines established by corporate conglomerates, and that demands a sophisticated sense of self-protection is one of the greatest problems for any actor. The subject can perhaps be best approached by examining differences between child-world behavior and adult-world behavior, principally these:

A child is rewarded for being good.
An adult is rewarded for being useful.

The difference here is fundamental. The "goodness" of a child is measured in how well he performs in specified and assigned tasks; he is rewarded with gold stars, PhD's, and pats on the back. The evaluation of the child is made by persons interested in the child's development— parents, teachers, and sometimes friends. The adult world has no such gratuitous assignments, and no such objective evaluations. If the casting director says "You're very talented," he simply feeds you a gold star that costs him nothing to give, and that might prevent you from bombing his apartment when he casts somebody else. The fact is, if they need you, they'll hire you; if they don't need you, they won't hire you, and for all your talent, your experience, your dedication, your awards, your recommendations, your good looks, your intelligence, and your magnificent audition, you are as pragmatically worthless as a comatose armadillo. This is the toughest of lessons, and it is routinely and ruthlessly administered.

If you suspect that all the foregoing information has been placed here to alarm you, your suspicions are correct. Later we will have some pleasanter things to say about acting as a profession, but at this point nothing would be more misleading than to encourage people into a profession that doesn't want them and has virtually no room for them. There is not a single producer, director, actor, or union executive who does not routinely advise aspiring actors "Don't bother." We pass on the same advice, knowing full well that the people who are going to transcend it will disregard us anyway.

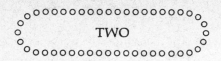
What you will need

If you are going to make it—that is, if you are going to make a livelihood as an actor—then you must possess the following:

Talent

A charming / fascinating / interesting / likable / hateful / definable personality

Certain physical characteristics

Proper training

Experience

Contacts

Commitment and will to succeed

A healthy attitude and capacity for psychological adjustment

Freedom from entanglements and inhibitions

Good information, advice, and help

Luck

Quite likely you rebel at seeing some of these items listed, such as "contacts," "certain physical characteristics," or "freedom from inhibitions." We do not mean these items in the usual melodramatic sense. You do not have to be the son of a cameraman, or a Miss Georgia contestant, and you certainly do not have to sleep with the casting director, to succeed in an acting career. But we stand firm on the importance of developing contacts, becoming flexible in your acting, and caring for your body. Without these interests you probably do not have the attitude requisite to becoming a performer. Considered singly, these are the basic ingredients for professional work.

Talent

We are happy to report that, after 20 years of study, we still find that the first requirement for success is talent. It is of incomparably greater importance than any other factor. Talent is the *sine qua non* of a performer. Certainly there are those who make a brief appearance on the professional scene without it, but lasting success comes only to those who have it. Do *you* have it? That is the question on which neuroses are based. Here are some basic guidelines for answering that question.

As a performer, you must be outstanding *now*. In college or neighborhood plays, you should be getting major roles or being considered for them. If after two or three years of training as an actor you still are unsuccessful at getting these roles in college or community theatre productions, you should reconsider. "Major" roles, of course, are not defined just by size, but as the roles you *want* to play—the roles you think you *ought* to play. While it may be perfectly true that "there are no small roles, only small actors," the fact remains that in a nonprofessional situation only a major role will fully expand and test your abilities. The size of a role is not of primary consequence; the depth, breadth, wit, passion, individuality, and "electricity" of the role: these are the characteristics that determine whether it is "major." A policeman who comes in at the end to arrest somebody, or Morton in *Henry IV* Part II, who describes at the beginning of the play everything that has happened since the end of Part I: these are certainly roles that can be played magnificently or badly, but in themselves they are hardly an accurate test of future potential.

The people we have seen rise to successful careers and even stardom in the past 20 years were without significant exception recognized as *extraordinarily* talented at the very beginning. While craft and experience can be acquired along the way, talent, where it exists, shows up almost immediately.

On the other hand, that extraordinary talent does not at all mean perfection of performance or anything even close to it. Extraordinarily talented people have been sunk in one disaster after another. They perform badly, they cannot be heard, they are not believable, they do the same thing over and over, they become too fat or too thin, they are always committing some terrible error or other, and they often reap the scorn of their peers and sometimes even of their directors. But they always get cast. Hardly anyone had a good thing to say about Stacy Keach when he was a student at Yale Drama School, for example. The other acting students gravely discussed his near-fatal problems, and his teachers despaired of his ability to grow under their tutelage. But he was cast in every leading male role available the year he was there, and he is now a stage and film star. His talent was so enormous that no director could turn him down when it came time to cast his play, and so obvious that it could only incite jealousy among his peers.

Extraordinary talent manifests itself in many ways. It is always accompanied by a great inner confidence: in fact, some say it is *only* that. Confidence is the power a person has over his own personality; it allows him to accept criticism and at the same time to rise above it. It allows him to believe in the reality of his own performance even when and if no one else does. An actor may have all kinds of doubts about his potential for career success, but he may not doubt that "he is an actor," that he can act. He must believe it in his bones. He must believe it in every interview and every audition, and believe it so much that his belief shows even though he makes no *effort* to show it. It is the power that makes him galvanize everything that he is as a person, and everything he has learned as an actor, into an exciting and apparently artless performance or audition.

"Talent is not definable, but it is recognizable." This is a common statement and it makes sense. Talent is variously described as magnetism, electricity, stage presence. We think it is those qualities that make a person *project without pushing*. Such "presence" carries through offstage as well as onstage: it involves the way you dress, talk, communicate, live, eat, and look. Onstage it involves your ability to communicate naturally with the simplest and most basic tools: speech, gesture, and body action. Because acting is basically an art that draws on the unconscious, an actor's *offstage* behavior often reveals "presence" as well. This is why we say that talent is frequently recognizable in daily life.

Personal magnetism or "electricity" is an aspect of talent. Magnetism is the capability of drawing others to yourself, of drawing others out and leading them with your words, your body, and your eyes. It is the capability of establishing rapport, and setting up mutual vibrations, both intellectually and emotionally. It is the capability of entering into mutual feedback with other actors, and with an audience as well.

If an actor has magnetism, he stands out in any performance, no matter how much of an amateur he may be. He is watched. He may make mistakes, but he is watched. And he is judged. He is great or terrible, he wears too much makeup, he is too effeminate, he is sensational, he is loud, he is incomprehensible, he is this or he is that—but he is never boring. Chances are we would like to meet him after the show, because he seems to be a fascinating person. He is talented.

If you have been in or around the theatre for a few years and nobody ever thought about you in this way, and if *you* have not thought about yourself in this way, then—we won't say this again—it is time to think of bricklaying or veterinary medicine.

Talent means all this and more still. It *can* mean, in addition:

• That a person sings, dances, juggles, tells jokes, or does striptease, backflips, handsprings, or T'ai Chi. Most talented people can do some of these; many more think they are talented because they can do one or two. A person who is genuinely talented need not be able to sing on key but can probably "sell" a song if called upon to do so. The more talents a person has in his portfolio, obviously, the more employable he is.

• That a person can communicate nuances clearly yet subtly. That he can vary inflection and timing so as to communicate what his director wants, without excessive coaching or reworking. Whether he does this by technique or instinct is not the concern of this book, but that he must be able to do it, everyone agrees. And he must be able to do it rapidly, particularly during an audition.

• That a person has a flexible, mobile, and expressive voice and body. These are the actor's tools. At the outset, the actor must be in possession of an expressive speaking voice: one that communicates what is between the lines, that connotes something beyond the mere words spoken. Similarly the talented person communicates in body movement and repose more than a mannequin. Sex appeal is obviously related to this, and although that is not by a long shot the whole story, it is clear that an audience sensually intrigued is an audience already on its way to admiring and relishing a performance. Casting directors have never been oblivious to this. You should not be, either.

• That a person stands out in a crowd, or a chorus, without seeming to try. Because of his energy, or his deep-set eyes, or the way he tosses his head, curls his lip, or studiously reflects, his presence alone draws attention. It is hard to imagine cultivating this quality in oneself. At the same time, it is such a quality that distinguishes certain people even when lined up at a ticket counter. Can one imagine not looking twice at Richard Burton, or Jacqueline Bisset, or Elliot Gould? It is not a matter of beauty necessarily, but of personal excitement.

• That a person is relaxed in front of others, or when performing for others, and enjoys such performing. This enjoyment is said to result from an exhibitionistic instinct, and nothing in our experience contradicts that. Though an actor may be as shy as anyone else—and not a few of them are painfully shy—some part of his personality relishes contact with others, even via the formal medium of theatre or film. The desire for fame need not be great, nor need there be a mammoth desire for great public or financial success. But there must be some strong, basic impulse toward reaching one's natural audience, small or large, and stimulating them.

These are all aspects of "talent," and the word is often used to denote one or more of them. There are no firm prerequisites for "making it" in show business, but the necessity for talent comes as close as any possibly could.

Personality

We list this second and there are shrieks. "What does my personality have to do with it? I'm an actor, not a prostitute! Use me for my talent—for what I can do; not for what I am! My personality is my own business!" Yes, it is, and your business is acting. As the American actor William Gillette said more than 60 years ago, "Among those elements of Life and Vitality, but greatly surpassing all others in importance, is the human characteristic or essential quality which passes under the execrated name of Personality. The very word must send an unpleasant shudder through this highly sensitive Assembly; for it is supposed to be quite the proper and highly cultured thing to sneer at Personality as an altogether cheap affair and not worthy to be associated for a moment with what is highest in Dramatic Art. Nevertheless, cheap or otherwise, inartistic or otherwise, and whatever it really is or not, it is the most singularly important factor for infusing the Life-Illusion into modern stage creations that is known to man."* Sixty years have not changed the import of Gillette's well-capitalized comments.

American film and theatre performances today are dominated by the Stanislavski/Strasberg/*cinéma verité* school of acting. Whether one is happy or sad about this, it remains true: so totally true that even directors and producers who publicly condemn "the method" nevertheless refuse to cast any actor who does not follow its basic precepts. They are, of course, unaware of this, but it is nonetheless true. Particularly in film and television work, the actor is cast largely on the basis of his "personal quality." The major casting decisions are made without, or before, auditions. For one role 50 actresses may be interviewed. The three or four who have the right "quality" for the role are then given copies of the text to read aloud for the producer. Thus, 92 percent of the decision is based on the candidate's personal behavior, and 8 percent on her talent and ability beyond that. Professional stage work is determined more by auditioning than interviewing, but the importance of a stageworthy personality—one suited to the role, of course—is still enormously great.

* *The Illusion of the First Time In Acting* (New York: Dramatic Museum of Columbia University, 1915), p. 45.

The reasons for this are many. Primarily, directors are seeking naturalness and they are commercially pressured to get it quickly. Unlike Stanislavski himself, the modern American stage director must get good characterizations in a matter of three or four weeks; the television director has at most a couple of days and frequently only about fifteen minutes. On a normal television shooting schedule, the actor will appear on the set, with his lines learned and ready to shoot, at eight o'clock in the morning. He has had no instructions whatever, has had the script for maybe twenty-four hours, and meets the director minutes before the actual shooting. There is a quick rehearsal, the blocking is set, and the director may give a reading or direction or two. Minutes later the scene is filmed and they are on to the next.* Clearly there is no time to work at developing a character. Television directors, therefore, *must* use your personality as a basis for casting. The foundation of this short-order work is simply Stanislavski's "Magic If." What would you do "if" you were Linda, the female bartender, in *All In the Family*, and Archie Bunker were yelling at you and your boyfriend were trying to get your attention? Linda will do it as *you* would do it, and Linda comes out looking a lot like you, which is why they cast you in the first place; that is how they saw Linda.

Acting in films and on the stage gives the actors and director more time to work out characterizations; still the premium, in this country, is on believability in portrayal. Casting directors tend to look for personal characteristics and idiosyncrasies that can be carried into the role. The film camera, which penetrates ruthlessly through all your high school and college "schtick" acting, comes up with the real you. If that is not what they want, you do not get the job. Even our stage acting is based on realism for the most part, particularly when compared to the European theatre. The development of *cinéma verité* in films and improvisational acting on stage has made this even more apparent in the 70's. And while no one could argue successfully that realism demands absolute fidelity to one's own personality, it certainly is true that what you have to start with in that regard is a major factor in the performance you will give.

---

* This is the schedule for a "day player" cast in a small role. Naturally, regular performers in a series will have more rehearsal time, but most television actors begin their careers as day players.

Nor is it sufficient simply to have a personality that is "right for the role." You must also have a widely appealing personality. One of the most frightening developments in television casting has been the recent introduction of the "TVQ," which is a tabulated "personality rating" of each performer on the screen—as established by surveys of families down to their six-year-old children. According to the Screen Actors Guild, "A low 'Q' score could spell disaster in a casting situation. Exclusion from the list can mean that a performer will not be considered for a major role on some television show. Many directors now find their first, second, and even third choices rejected because of a low Q or no Q." This even extends, in some cases, to day players. Some sample Q scores are included in the Appendix, and while the acting unions are working to reduce the importance of this product-marketing approach to acting, its influence is more likely to grow and extend than to disappear.

What is a good acting personality? It is no one thing in particular, but it is something definable in general terms. You are shy, you are fascinating, you are profound, you are aggressive, you are hostile, you are nasty, you are fiery, you are sensual, you are youthful, you are idealistic, you are wacky, you are serene. Plain ordinary old NICE will get you nowhere. Thousands of aspiring actors have "blown" an interview simply by being polite and forgotten. Yes, there is an "interview technique." A hundred actors will explain, "I didn't get the job because I don't play their games at the interview. I'm just not that kind of person." But it's not a game. Interview technique is simply letting them see just *what* kind of person you *are*. If that is hidden behind a lot of "pleased-to-meet-yous" and "thank-you-very-muches," you will find not only that you have lost your chance at a further audition, but that you have in fact been playing *your own* game—the parents' and teachers' and business school's interview game—and that for perhaps the first time in your life it was the wrong game to play. The casting game is the business of projecting (for you) and discovering (for them) your real self, whatever that may be.

Successful actors are not bland people. That is not to say that they are brash, either. Most of our acquaintance are people of depth, sensitivity, dedication, and artistry. Their personalities are not applied for the sake of calling attention to themselves. The surest way to lose your personality is to fake one. Your real personality will follow you in every role you play; it will become your trademark. In the classic days of Hollywood such trademarks were Bogart's toughness, John Wayne's reckless virility, Fonda's sensitive passion, Marilyn Monroe's soft, defenseless sexuality, Marlon Brando's vulnerable egotism, W. C. Fields's cynicism, Mae West's leering defiance, Grace Kelly's poise, and Clark Gable's cockiness. These were not "put on" personalities, they were intrinsic to their owners and vital to their success. The personalities of today's rising stars are more subtle, perhaps, but just as ingrained in their performances, even in varied characterizations. One need only remember Dustin Hoffman's defensive smirk in *The Graduate* and *Midnight Cowboy* or Elliot Gould's whining snarl in *M*A*S*H* and *California Split*. The day of the "personality actor" is far from over; in fact there is no indication that it is even beginning to end.

You cannot create your personality—your stage personality—but you can liberate it. What are your personal characteristics? What do others see in you? Find out and let those characteristics come out. Do not worry about "your good features versus your bad features." Just have features. Don't be afraid to be different. Don't opt for the ordinary, for the nice. Don't try to be what you think they want you to be. Don't worry about yourself. Be proud of yourself. Like yourself. If you do not, it is hard to see how somebody else will.

One more aspect of personality deserves your attention, one so obvious that most young actors completely ignore it: Does the director like you personally? There should be nothing surprising about this; like everyone else, directors want to enjoy their work, and they would rather work with people they like than with people they don't like. They are, in short, just like you. There is an artistic component to this principle as well; filmmaker William Bayer advises would-be directors who are casting a film that, after extensive auditions, "in the end the most important quality to look for in an actor may be rapport: are you going to be able to work with this actor on a basis of intimate friendship? When a film is shooting and the pressure is on, friendship and understanding may be the qualities that have most to do with failure or success."* While there is no assured way of generating that

---

* *Breaking Through, Selling Out, Dropping Dead* (New York: Macmillan, 1971), p. 38.

rapport, you should be able to recognize its importance, and open yourself up to it without feeling guilty. Perhaps it is safe to say that if you are the kind of person who combines vivacity with sensitivity, and sincerity with charm, then you might be the kind of person a director would like to choose for his company—and his company.

Physical characteristics

No cry in the theatre is raised as strongly as that against "type casting." The art of acting, it is often maintained, is the actor's ability to essay a wide range of roles of varying ages, historical periods, dramatic characteristics, and styles. Repertory, it is said, encourages actors to alternate between Molière comedy, Tennessee Williams romanticism, and Shakespearean tragedy—from the youthful Romeo to the aged Northumberland. No doubt. But most casting in the professional theatre and in film and TV today is done by physical type. Until that changes the following advice should be of value.

Your physical type begins with your race and your sex, neither of which is ordinarily expected to be altered by theatrical make-up. While Laurence Olivier may be cast as a Moorish general and Judith Anderson as a Danish prince, these cases stem from the fame of the individuals rather than any policy of fair employment practices. In fact, the acting profession is and will continue to remain racist and sexist long after most of these words have lost their timeliness, for racial and sexual discrimination are at the very heart of the casting process. The burdens of this situation weigh heaviest on women, for while they may comprise up to three-fourths of the university students enrolled in acting classes, they will receive only about one-third to one-fourth of the acting roles available professionally. One might say that although the status of women in the theatre has certainly improved since the Renaissance, when they were not permitted to perform at all, it hasn't improved much. In repertory theatres, women ordinarily comprise no more than one-third of an acting company, and on television and films their ratio to men may even be slimmer. The Women's Conference Committee of SAG has pointed out that under SAG contracts male employment outnumbers female employment 5 to 1 in the 35–45 age range, which contains the majority of starring roles. On television commercials men outnumber women 2 to 1 and seize a gigantic 93 percent of the "voice-overs" (off-camera speaking roles). Minorities (racial and national) have made strong gains recently, but the percentage of minorities employed, particularly in leading roles, remains well behind the percentages they represent of the American population.

It should not be assumed that this racism and sexism are merely a reflection of bigotry on the part of directors or producers. In the case of repertory theatres, the sexual ratio of players is dictated by the casts of characters these companies must fill. A typical Shakespearean play, for example, will have 15 to 25 men and 3 to 5 women. *St. Joan* has one female part in a cast of about two dozen; this may indicate medieval sexism or Shavian sexism, but it does not necessarily imply the same for the company choosing to produce *St. Joan*. And while interracial casting has broken many barriers in recent years, it is still not universally successful. In a production of Strindberg's *Dance of Death*, for example, the Tyrone Guthrie Theatre took the socially advanced step of casting a black actor and a white actress as brother and sister, only to force the audience into entirely gratuitous speculation about which one was illegitimate. Experimental casting, both interracial and intersexual, has yet to achieve a major impact on paying, professional acting situations.

Your race and sex, then, are largely unchangeable. The same applies to your age, your size, and your bone structure. However, your weight, dress, state of health, posture, hair style, complexion, and grooming give you great latitudes for control. What should you aim for in these?

As with personality, there is no classic norm. The ideal of perfect beauty, nowadays, is as worthless as the "nice" personality, and the waiting rooms of New York and Hollywood casting offices are filled with hundreds of hopeless beauties from the charm schools, beauty contests, and super-elegant men's shops of America. As with personality, the premium is on a specific, *memorable* and *definable* "look" and that look should be within a specific time-honored "type."

Types exist, and they exist today exactly as they were a hundred years ago: male and female "children," "young leading men," "ingenues," "leading men," "leading women," "character men and comedians," and "character women and comediennes." There are subgroups, but these eight remain the basic ones. The *Players' Directory*, which is a publication of photographs of all working actors in the Los Angeles area, and an invaluable tool in the casting process, divides actors into these categories for the convenience of producers. If you aren't in the right category, you won't even be looked at.

"Children" designates actors 12 years old and younger. "Pre-teens" are those from 13 to 15, and "teens" from 16 to 19. Ordinarily these character types are not involved in romantic affairs. On stage, anyway.

"Ingenues" (girls) and "young leading men" are in the "first love" category. Usually they are in their early to mid-twenties and send off vibrations of youth, innocence, and charm.

"Leading men" and "leading ladies" are, by contrast, wiser, more experienced lovers; glamorous, romantic, mature, sophisticated, in their mid-twenties to mid-forties and beyond.

"Character men," "character women," "comedians," and "comediennes" are not romantic in a conventional sense. They are usually older, and their appearance is likely to be distinctive rather than attractive.

Notice that types are not defined solely by age, but also by a position on some sort of sexual scale. This is simply an accurate reading of the typing that is done in theatre and film casting. No one assumes that an unattractive character cannot be portrayed in a romantic role (as in *Marty*). It is just that to do so is to cast deliberately against type, and such casting is rarely done except when a specific play or film calls for it. Since the time of Aristophanes, audiences have expected ingenues to be young and innocent, lovers to be beautiful and sensitive, and comics to be old and usually pudgy. Few casting directors wish to disappoint an audience.

It is important to find your type, if only to get yourself in the right chapter of the *Players' Guide*. More than that, you are categorized in the producer's mind; you are provided with a convenient label—a basis for comparison with other actors. You protest: you are an individual, not a type! If you are Laurence Olivier, you do not need a label. If you are not, you must start somewhere. Even "male" or "female" is a label, and you can be at least a little more specific than that.

You must decide whether you can play juveniles, for example. Either you can play fourteen-year-olds or you cannot. Perhaps you can do a passable job, of course, but can you do better than a *real* fourteen-year-old? If so, sign up, because producers hate to use real fourteen-year-olds if they can avoid it. (They really hate to use anybody younger than eighteen, because they must pay to have a tutor on the set. If you are nineteen and can play twelve, they will love you.)

You should clearly be a character actor or not. If you are ten pounds overweight, you are dead. Either lose it, or gain twenty more. If you look like an IBM executive or a nineteen-year-old groupie you are fine, but if you look half like one and half like the other, you are in trouble. If you are ugly, don't worry about hiding it. Cultivate it. Use what you have to create a distinctive appearance. Be happy with what you are. Make it count. One of the most successful young actors today has a prominent hare-lip scar and was half bald at 29. Neither has been masked by surgery or Hair-Anew. There is no "bad" appearance except a bland, characterless, typeless one.

For leading men and women, the old ideals are out the window. It is no longer necessary for men to be tall, dark, and handsome, or for women to be platinum blondes with hourglass figures. Certain looks "come in" from time to time: urban ethnic (Dustin Hoffman, Elliot Gould, Al Pacino, Richard Dreyfuss, Woody Allen) has been a peculiarly dominant look for young leading men in recent years, while gamine-like pertness (Mia Farrow, Kim Darby, Goldie Hawn) and earthy frankness (Maria Schneider, Ellen Burstyn, Gena Rowlands), seem to have replaced the bosomy voluptuousness that characterized the young leading women of the past; these "looks" can be cultivated, and in fact *have* been cultivated by most if not all of the actors who exhibit them. The specifics of personal physical appearance are not individually important; what counts is the effect that your person and your "image" create, and the power of that effect, which should be enormous. If you are a leading man, you must appeal to women; woman, vice versa. There are all kinds of ways of doing that, and for some it comes more naturally than for others. But you *can* do it if you're willing to devote some time, a little money, and a frankly self-critical attitude to the problem. The main difference between professional and amateur theatre auditions, it seems to us, is the total lack of concern amateurs have over their personal appearance. They are simply blind to the realities, and often appear to be waiting for some Star of Bethlehem to shine over them and so point them out to the director. The folly of this approach need not be further discussed.

Cultivate distinction in appearance. Separate yourself from the rest of your friends. Find an exciting hairstyle for yourself, a natural one if that is the current trend, but one that looks better on you than on anybody else, and that is not seen too much. Dress distinctively. If you are a girl and you like going around in jeans and body shirts, then get some that fit right, and some great belts and boots, and look terrific. Extravagance and propriety are not worth a plugged nickel in this business, but distinction *in your own terms* is. Find yourself, and find in yourself a unique appearance that will intrigue others.

One necessary word about your weight, however. If you should lose weight, do so. Most Americans are overweight. Most performers are not. There is a rather direct correlation between chubby actors and those who do not get work. Particularly in film and television, where the camera adds ten or fifteen pounds to you anyway, the premium is and has always been on slim, lissome people. Take a look at the young people playing the three-line parts on television programs. Are they fat? No. These are the parts you will be going for if you're just starting out. This becomes even more true if you are offering yourself as a dancer or singer. Flip Wilson and Kate Smith are rarities, and not for general emulation. Unless you are completely sure you want to make it as a fat character actor, take off those extra 20 pounds, cinch in your waist, and do not worry if your parents wonder why you are so skinny. The Bieler diet and the so-called "water diet" are favorites among actors for quick and lasting weight loss.

How do you *use* your appearance? It precedes you in every interview and every audition. Your photographs are your letters of introduction. No actor can begin to look for work without a set of photographs, and so we have a separate section on the subject. Read it thoroughly in conjunction with this one. Your photographs should show just what your appearance should show: originality, vitality, distinctiveness. If you look like something out of a high school yearbook, the chances are that you will never be heard of again.

Training and experience

You need it. No matter how naturally talented, attractive, sexy, and individual you are, you will flop in the audition if you don't know what to do. In the old days, a decade or more ago, actors without formal training were the rule. As Hermione Gingold once said, "I got all the schooling any actress needs. That is, I learned to write enough to sign contracts."* Now this sort of attitude has become very definitely the exception. Training in the art and craft of acting is a virtual necessity for a successful career, and if you *are* hired at first without it, you will need it thereafter. There are six major sorts of training you may take: high school drama classes, college drama or film classes, commercial acting classes, studio classes, apprenticeships, or private instruction. Each of these groups is populated with enough master teachers and inspiring creative artists to train a cast of thousands.

Good teachers pop up in the craziest places, and there is no reason why a high school drama class cannot be a stimulating and effective training program. Some undoubtedly are. Frequently high schools are fortunate in hiring out-of-work (or given-up-in-disgust) professional actors who transmit their knowledge masterfully to eager young people. That is a good start. And there are many fine drama programs in colleges across the country that provide basic training in acting as well as in other theatre skills and subjects. Yale University, Carnegie-Mellon University, Catholic University, New York University, USC, and UCLA have developed, over the years, fine reputations within the professional theatre and professional film worlds. Many more universities in the American heartland have also built reputations over the years: Michigan, Wayne State, Indiana, Oklahoma, Texas, Colorado, Washington, Missouri, Florida, North Carolina, Cornell, and Syracuse, to name a few. Some of the best of these schools have recently organized into the League of Professional Training Programs, whose curricula and instruction are scrutinized by outside professional examiners, and whose offerings are modeled on the conservatory approach. The League is headquartered at the School of the Arts at New York University, where further information is available. And while college graduates ten years ago may have sought to hide their diplomas from theatrical employers, they now may proudly sport not only BA's but MA's, MFA's, and even PhD's without embarrassment. For as we shall see, the professional theatre and film world has moved into an informal alliance with the

---

* William Fadiman, *Hollywood Now* (New York: Liveright, 1972), p. 82.

universities, and while the old resentments occasionally persist, the two worlds have moved into a closer proximity.

Why is this? For one reason, most Americans go to college now, and those college students who plan to be actors now study drama instead of chemistry or political science. Drama, which has been introduced as a subject of legitimate study only in the last 40 years, is now a "major" on literally hundreds of campuses, and graduate degrees in Theatre, Theatre Arts, Filmmaking, Drama, and Dramatic Art are now commonplace.

Secondly, the "educational theatre" establishment has itself become much more professionalized, and experienced professional actors and directors are being sought eagerly to provide on-campus instruction. Many university drama departments, in fact, suffer a split between the professionally oriented faculty, and the older, academically oriented one. It is imperative that prospective students determine the climate in the drama department of their choice before signing on: they may find that students and professors interested in professional theatre or film work are discriminated against in favor of prospective speech teachers and Racine scholars.

Thirdly, the professional theatre has to some extent become more "educationalized." Films in this country are now a relevant reflection of culture and ideas. Successful films are more and more directed toward philosophical and social ends. Television has experimented with "relevance," and even if that experiment has disappointed most critics, the general level of all media entertainment has become more thoughtful than in past decades. A simple comparison of *Lucas Tanner* and *Room 222* (1970's) to *Our Miss Brooks* (1960's) or *Mister Peepers* (1950's) proves the point. Furthermore, educational television, public broadcasting, and subsidized regional theatre experimentation call for intelligent, broadly trained actors as well as a college-level audience.

So college experience, and college experience in drama or a drama-related discipline, while not essential, has become at least a desirable part of an actor's training. A degree is sometimes helpful, and a graduate degree sometimes more helpful, although it is hard to ascertain this by actual records. But it is also true that no one has ever been denied a role because he lacked a college degree.

Should you go to college? If you are in college, should you stay?

Should you go on to graduate school? These are vital questions for many students.

In general, if you are planning a career as a professional actor, you might follow these precepts:

If you have graduated from high school, desire to go to college, and have been accepted at a college with a good drama department, go. Major in drama and act in every play you can. If the college has a film department, get involved there too.

Stay in college as long as you feel you are really growing as an actor. Measure this on a year-to-year, not day-to-day, basis.

If at any time in your college career six or eight months pass during which you feel you have got everything out of the college that you can, that you have surpassed most of the other students in your talent and craft, and that the directors and instructors do not have much left to teach you and are not inspiring you, think about leaving.

If you feel ready to take the professional plunge, do so. You will never be more ready.

If, however, you still wish to get your degree, see if you can transfer to a big metropolitan campus such as NYU, UCLA, USC, or CUNY and finish your degree work while trying to get involved professionally on the side. This is hazardous and full of problems, but it beats wasting another year or two around the old quad redoing your old character-izations. At least you will be thrown into another crowd and forced up against fresh competition and criticism.

If, having received your BA in drama, you still feel the need of further academic training and a higher degree, go to graduate school. But beware. Graduate schools are full of persons without the will to commit toward a career. By now you should know whether you want to go for a professional career or a teaching career. Indecision at this point could blow your chances for either. However, if you wish to con-tinue working toward the profession while getting an MFA at the same time, we offer some suggestions:

Go to the very best graduate school you can. Ask your teachers what they are: they vary from time to time.

Go to a graduate school within commuting distance of New York or Los Angeles, or with a direct contact with a professional regional theatre. No matter how fine a school may be in Kansas or Alaska, you will leave there with your PhD in hand at 26 and be miles behind a 16-year-old graduate of Hollywood High or New York's High School of Performing Arts.

Work for the work, not for the degree. Learn everything you can, not just what you're told to learn or made to learn. Don't be satisfied with being good (or worse, "good enough,"). Be *great*. As one actor puts it, "Acting is a champion business—people here are very into champions." So risk total failure with the knowledge that you have nothing to lose and everything to gain. The degree itself is not your goal, and should not be in the way of your goal. As Joseph Papp (director of the New York Shakespeare Festival Theatre) points out, "In New York, a PhD won't get you through the turnstile of the IRT (subway)." But what you *learn* en route to an advanced degree may.

Do not ever forget that you are trying to enter the most competitive profession that exists, and that only the very best academic credentials mean anything whatever.

The foregoing only applies to students planning professional careers. In another chapter we discuss adequate preparation for teaching careers, which is naturally quite different.

What does a college education do for you? As far as your dramatic instruction, it is probably going to be pretty good. Some colleges have fine acting instructors with whom you may study regularly for your entire four-year academic career. Others allow you to study acting only for a year or two, but then give you credit for workshop plays and major productions. Many give you professional direction, and others let you work with regional companies and actually play roles in professional productions. Virtually all the major colleges have facilities for theatrical production that make professional producers livid with envy; 80-dimmer 10-preset electronic lighting boards that far surpass Broadway standards are common on campus stages. Generally the equipment in the colleges is advanced beyond anything you may work with for the rest of your life—even if you make it.

Does a college degree help you get a job? Yes and no. Or rather, no and yes, because the negative somewhat outweighs the positive. No New York or Hollywood producer will ask you for evidence of a college degree or even a college education, and few actors even bother to list their degrees on their professional resumes. But producers and directors do want to know you can act, and college acting experience, if they like you to begin with, is helpful, if not impressive. In fact, a college degree may be your ultimate tool in breaking into the union. Present Screen Actors' Guild regulations require the producer to pay a $250 fine* for casting a non-union actor in a film role, unless that actor can prove that he is "equivalently trained." A college degree in drama, together with a letter of recommendation from a drama professor, is accepted evidence that the student is a genuinely dedicated actress, for example, and not simply a starstruck barmaid from last night's post-production bash.

Finally, it is through college drama departments that young actors may get their first job, via the intermediate step of Theatre Communications Group (TCG) auditions. The TCG auditions, supplemented now by the University Resident Theatre Association auditions (both are described later), are held each year to bring together the best university drama students with directors of regional theatres. They are an important step for many actors, and accessible for the most part only to graduates of college drama programs.

On the other hand, a disadvantage of college theatres is that the amateur level is rarely surpassed. Principal performers can be excellent, but depth in casting is almost always lacking. The commonest problem is finding student actors capable of playing mature and old character parts. Pushing young actors into these roles creates a standard that perforce accepts "phony" acting, and lowers the overall production level. Too much work under these conditions allows actors and directors to assume lower standards and routinely excuse sloppy, amateurish work—or worse, to admire it, since "under the circumstances" it is all that can be achieved. If this is carried through to acting styles as a whole, then the college experience can be a disastrous one. The professionally oriented student actor (or director) in colleges must refuse to be dragged down by the amateurism and lack of commitment, of real talent, and of perfectionism that will in many cases surround him.

However, beyond the basic dramatic instruction, college in general offers many hidden advantages that are important to the young actor. A college education is a genuinely humanizing, broadening experience.

* That's the fine for casting a non-union day player. For a weekly player the fine is $500.

It can introduce the actor to literature, history, psychology, politics, philosophy, economics, sociology, and the other arts and sciences that will be invaluable to him in his work. As an artist, the actor should also be a thoughtful, aware person. As Duncan Ross, Artistic Director of the Seattle Repertory Theatre, says, "There is no such thing as a good actor who is unintelligent—by any appropriate definition of the term." That is one reason why so many of them are becoming involved in political and social action. The days of the "dumb blonde" and the "stupid stud" are past; today's actors, while not necessarily intellectuals, know how to think. They often branch out into writing, producing, directing, and even politics. No one should skip or leave college *merely* out of impatience for a career, nor should a young actor, while enrolled in college, limit himself strictly to acting courses and school plays. It is not necessary to examine every course in the college catalogue for its immediate importance or relevance to acting. The important thing is to learn, and to learn as much as you can about everything. It can't hurt, and it will probably help.

College, however, is only one form of education. There are hundreds of young actors without the money, the interest, or even the intelligence to go to college and for them, *and* for college dropouts, there are several noncollegiate alternatives. Principally there are commercial acting schools and studios. A few are listed in the Appendix to this book, but a full list is available in the Los Angeles and New York yellow pages. (It is almost totally useless to go to a commercial school anywhere else, no matter how good it is, except for your own entertainment.)

Commercial schools vary enormously according to the interest of the instructor in his students and also according to his ability. Some, with famous names, are so past their usefulness that their classes are painful; others, both famous and unknown, can be inspiring. Get recommendations from anybody you know: a personal interview or personal reference is probably the best possible way of locating a good instructor. But all commercial schools can be as good as the amount of work you are willing to do. You pay your money, you do your assignments, and you listen to the instructor. Just working with other professionally minded students is extremely helpful. *All* aspiring actors, no matter what their prior training, should, if they can afford it, enroll ιn a good regular commercial acting class as soon as they hit New York or Los Angeles. For many, it's the first step into developing talent and contacts; for all, it is a way of continuing to grow in that long period before the first job or two.

In private instruction, one teacher works with students either singly or in small groups. Union office bulletin boards, trade journals, and occasionally the yellow pages list these along with larger acting schools. Many professional actors retain the regular services of an acting coach long after they become rich and famous; many have specialized coaches for acting, singing, voice, speech, and so on. Hiring a coach or signing on for private instruction is more expensive than taking an advertised class, and less valuable in terms of introducing you to large numbers of people. But if you can get with a coach who has a well-known clientele (and who is called upon, from time to time, by casting directors) you may have found yourself a very good deal.

You must, of course, use extreme care in choosing a commercial school or private teacher. Some offer the finest acting instruction available anywhere. The Neighborhood Playhouse School of the Theatre, the HB studio (run by the splendid team of Herbert Berghof and Uta Hagen), the Lee Strasberg Institute: these and many others have sent hundreds of well-trained, superior actors into the profession. Others, unfortunately, are clip joints, pure and simple. The larger commercial schools have some placement services, but beware of any school or class that implies a job guarantee upon graduation. The courts are always after these people who advertise "Big pay, glamour await you!" and then soft-sell you for $465 (half the regular price, because you are so talented) for what amounts to a twenty-hour acting course taught by someone who once knew a Mousketeer. These schools, until they are shut down by the authorities, prey on the ignorance and fantasies of young actors and their families. It is easy to check the reliability of any school or acting coach, and local unions, agents, actors, and even the Better Business Bureau can provide information. Disbelieve all "too good to be true" promises: they are just that.

Apprenticeship with a repertory or summer stock company is a supremely good way of gaining theatre training, and this may supplement other forms of education. Various programs combine collegiate experience with professional repertory experience: for example, the

Bush Fellowships involve study at the University of Minnesota and performance with the Minnesota (Tyrone Guthrie) Theatre Company, and the MFA program at Florida State University is associated with the fine Asolo Theatre of Sarasota. Apprenticeships with repertory companies are not easy to get, but summer stock apprenticeships are fairly easy to come by, and if you are good enough, you may end up with an Equity card in the process. Summer theatres, most of which are on the East Coast, and primarily in New England, are companies of professional actors that perform regularly for local and resort crowd audiences. Apprentices usually pay room, board, and a small tuition; live with the company; perform various backstage duties; and are occasionally permitted to perform small roles. The theatrical training is extraordinarily good for those who dedicate themselves to getting the most out of it, and frequently apprentices become full company members in succeeding years. The union regulations allow a summer stock producer to cast an apprentice an unlimited number of times in his first season with the company, but in his second year with the company, he must be signed to an Equity contract for his fourth role. An apprentice cannot remain with the company for a third year without being signed to Equity. There is some misunderstanding of this principle; merely being with a summer stock company for three years does not make you Equity; a summer stock producer has to want you so badly for the fourth production of your second year that he is willing to hire you at Equity wages (instead of getting you for free, as he has for the previous year and a half). If he does not want you that much, he simply will not cast you. But do not let this bother you. The training in working for a professional company is more than enough compensation. It is more than training; it is invaluable experience.

There is one final word to say about preprofessional training and experience. It can be overdone. College, acting classes, and the local community theatre can be very comfortable places. A lovely security envelops you—you are known, liked, respected, and well reviewed by the locals and by your teachers. But check your goals. If you want to move on, you had better go when you are ready rather than hang around merely because it is safe. Recognize the point of stagnation when the competition gets soft. There are actors who become so devoted to a favorite drama school or drama teacher that they study for eight or ten years without going out for a single audition, on the grounds that they are "not ready." The "professional student" is really psychologically aberrant. Recognize this trait in yourself, if it exists, and fight it. When you are ready to take the plunge, take it. The proper time is something only you can decide upon.

Contacts

Here we are. Contacts are the nemesis of the young unknown actor. You can whine, gripe, yell, and complain about it, but contacts are important—vital—in getting jobs in the theatre. But do not just quit on this account: *think*. What does the term "contacts" actually mean?

Contacts are the people you know and who know you. If you were casting a play in a hurry and knew someone who was "just right" for the role, wouldn't you call him up and offer him a chance to audition? Would you really search through the drama classes at State University to find out if there were somebody else as good or better? No. You would call Harry and say, "Harry, I've got a part that's just right for you." And Harry would come over and read it, and if you liked his reading you would cast him in the role. It is not that you owe Harry a favor, but you like him, you envision him doing the part, and you can settle the matter in a quick, friendly way. Well, maybe you are the one in a thousand who would not call Harry, but the other 999 are in New York and Hollywood casting offices right now. You can either moan about it or work to beat it: the choice is yours.

So there is nothing mysterious about "contacts," and it is fruitless to play the sour grapes routine and say "I can't get anywhere because I don't have any pull." Of course you don't, but neither does anybody else just starting out. It is not as though your competition all went to school with Jerry Lewis's kids or swam in Dinah Shore's pool. Everybody, or almost everybody, starts off just as unknown and unwanted as you. If you do not have contacts, you simply have to develop them. It is as simple as that.

But wait a minute, you say. You don't believe in "It's not *what* you know but *who* you know." You want to make it "on your own." What does that mean? That you will be discovered? Where? At acting class? Singing in the shower? NOBODY ever made it "on his own." It always takes somebody else, and that somebody is your contact. This is no time to play around with semantics. Getting jobs in theatre involves getting people to know you and know your work. These are your contacts, and if you are good enough, and develop enough of them, one of them will pay off for you. And then it does not matter if you got introduced because he was your uncle's cousin or your drama teacher's drama teacher. He saw you, he liked you, and he hired you. How else did you expect it to happen?

The fact is that most hirings in the theatre and film world is done among acquaintances and friends: not *all* of it, but *most* of it. Obviously directors would rather work with actors they have used before more than those they have never seen, all else being equal—and most of the time all else *is* equal. Similarly, most producers and casting directors are difficult to attract to showcase productions when total strangers are inviting them. If a producer knows you, he is more apt to drive to New Milford or Burbank Community Theatre to see you perform, and that means he is more likely to hire you.

And now, who said you have no contacts? Everybody you know is a potential contact. The actor in the community play with you might next year be producing a film; your college drama instructor might be directing a play; your uncle might have a friend who has just written a TV show. It is to your advantage to get to know people in the business; who knows what they might be doing in a month or so? Acquaintances of ours mail postcards to everyone they know every four or six months, just to stay in touch. It is not presumptuous: it is appreciated, and they get work.

The important contacts you presumably do not know yet, but you will. Every time you audition you meet at least one. At every interview you meet secretaries and other actors. These meetings can be forgotten in an instant, but if you are personable and they are intrigued by you, a contact is made. A word of caution: don't be pushy. Phony friendliness and phony friends are the most loathsome aspect of show business, and it is easy to completely misplay your hand in this way. Theatre people are the worst name-droppers in the world, and "Oh, he's a good friend of mine," becomes a line that is too frequently applied to a person met once five years ago. But you can build your real contacts—the people who know you and know your work—by simply and modestly finding ways to keep them aware of you. And you can keep aware of *them*, by writing down the name of everyone you meet in a little black book so that the next time you see them you can remember their names and what they do.

Remember these principles about contacts:

No one contact is going to make it for you, and the fact that somebody else knows somebody important is not going to make it for *him*, either. All the people you know can help you—and themselves—by trading information, tips, advice, and ultimately, offers of employment.

People you have known for years and who have subsequently "made it" may not help you out at all. That is not just because success has made them indifferent to their old pals. Many genuinely try to follow the suggestion of Edith Piaf, who said that when you reach the top you should throw the ladder back down for everybody else. But your newly arrived friends are not as secure as they seem. In fact, they are in a particularly vulnerable position. Even if they can help you they may not want to risk suggesting you to *their* superior, fearing that if you fail, they may fall. Beyond this, they may question their earlier evaluation of you now that they have new surroundings and a new perspective. They would rather you made it on your own: then they could be *sure*. This is small comfort, of course, but you will probably have to live with it.

Contacts may not look like contacts. The mousy-looking man hanging around backstage might just be getting ready to film *Godfather III* in Portuguese, and is looking you over for a part. Be yourself and make friends; it cannot hurt you.

Contacts may not act like contacts. People who give out jobs in show business are so besieged they frequently hide the fact behind a veil of feigned clumsiness and innocence. Play along.

All kinds of people will *tell* you that they are contacts. They're probably not. Maybe they are just nice and want to help, and maybe they are after your body. Some just like to sound important. Treat everybody the same, and do not be too sure of anyone.

A word about sleeping with the producer. If you are a talented, personable, with-it, sexy person, there will be all sorts of people anxious to cast you. There will also be all sorts of people interested in going to bed with you. They may not be the same people, however. Undoubtedly several will want to cast you *and* sleep with you, and several more will want nothing to do with you. There seems to be little correlation.

A cartoon hanging outside the Screen Gems casting office window shows a young girl dressing in a bedroom and calling to an older man, "Now, when are you going to make me a star?" The older man is in the next room, smiling and cutting her a paper star.

Now it is illogical to assume that if the casting director is your "steady," he won't be working a little harder for you than for the average woman who comes in for an interview, and it is equally obvious that if your bedpartner is a studio executive, all things are not going to be equal. We have already mentioned the strings that were pulled to get a well-bedded actress into *The Steagle*, but we should also note that once shooting was under way, and the woman proved disastrous, she was fired—with the net result much poorer for her than if she had not been hired in the first place. The point is that nobody gets a job *simply* by going from one studio bed or office couch to another. No producer makes that kind of deal; too much money is at stake, and too many people are ready to axe *him* if you are not good enough. And, quite frankly, there's a lot of sex available for a lot less risk. If you go to bed with anybody, don't expect anything but a good time.

In fact, the sexual politics of the acting industries is infinitely more subtle and fascinating than the old clichés about Broadway casting couches and Hollywood moguls chasing starlets through the backlot. Of course, there are producers, agents, and conglomerate accounts whose fantasies ignite when they contemplate the power they have and the oversupply of beautiful young people subject to that power; one casting director recently resigned because, he said, he was tired of pimping for his producer. But sexual trade-offs are rarely proposed directly, and are rarely if ever explicit. Perhaps, as it is often said, there is no more sexual dealing in show business than in the washing machine business or any other business—only it is simply more gossiped about in the general news media. We know of one young, uninhibited, and absolutely beautiful young actress who went out on 75 interviews in her first year in Hollywood without receiving a single overt pass. She did receive a few roles and performed well in them. "The passes come after you're hired," she said. She also related the adventure of a competitor who came to a screen test wearing the tiniest miniskirt and no underwear. Not only did this fail to get her the part—our friend got it—the infuriated director kicked her off the lot.

Commitment and will to succeed

This is your power supply. It keeps you going despite the thousand and one ego reversals you are bound to encounter. As a young professional actor explains, the greatest danger you face is going "DEAF— depressed, envious, aching, and frustrated." It is your commitment and sheer persistence that will vanquish DEAFness if anything can, that will keep you going through poverty and loneliness, when your friends are marrying and having kids and making money and you are eating out of cans on the Lower East Side waiting for your ship to come in. You must continue to hang in there, to train yourself, to get information and develop contacts, to do all the things you must. To do all these things, you must have an overwhelming desire for success. It is often said that the people who make it in the theatre are simply those who want it badly enough.

It is not necessary to step on other people's toes, to do zany things that draw attention to yourself, or to alienate friends, relatives, and competitors in your quest for success. But quest for it you must. Getting started in theatre means *initiating* actions: getting on the telephone and on the pavement, looking up people, calling on strangers, getting to places at 6 a.m. and waiting around for three hours—all sorts of indelicate and unappetizing tasks. It also means weeks, months, even years of frustration, failure, defeat, and simple boredom. It means sitting around waiting for the telephone to ring when it has not rung in months. These things are at best unpleasant and at worst lead you to the brink of suicidal depression. Only a massive will to succeed will overcome them. The commitment must be strong, persistent, and all-encompassing. All sorts of personal sacrifices simply must be assumed.

Nobody knows how long it will take to "make" you an actor. It is best to set yourself some sort of time schedule—most actors do. Three years is an average allotment: three years after the first day that you say to yourself, "I am now an actor, and I'm available for work." Three years from the day you hit the pavements, the studios, the agencies— from the day you decide that whatever you are doing, you will drop it to get the first job.

From that first day on, your commitment to your career must come first. If you are married, your spouse had better understand, or you are in trouble. If you are in college, you had better be ready to drop out. If you have a job, you had better be ready—and able—to resign. For the next three years—or whatever period you set for yourself—you are going for it, and you will do what is necessary to get it.

From that day on, you scrimp on money for gifts, for food, for furniture, for an apartment. You spend money on pictures, a telephone service, résumés, classes, and some good clothes for auditions. You get the sleep you need and the medication you need; you're going to have to be ready to look terrific on an hour's notice any day of the week. You direct your time, your money, and your energy to two things: learning acting and getting work, and whatever is left over goes to less important things like your social life or your marriage. You will not always like this, of course, but if you do not do it you will fall behind. When the odds are stacked against you to begin with, who can afford to fall? If you aren't 100 percent committed, you will simply lose the job to someone who is.

A committed attitude carries with it something more than a pragmatic advantage in selling yourself on the job market. Exciting people are committed people, in art, in politics, or in life. And it is to your advantage to be exciting. So be dedicated; it will offend the weak, but it will inspire others. A life of dedication (to your art, hopefully, but even to yourself) is fulfilling; it galvanizes your talents and directs your energies. It characterizes all great artists of all times. As Bernard Shaw wrote:

"This is the true joy in life, the being used for a purpose recognized by yourself as a mighty one: the being thoroughly worn out before you are thrown on the scrap heap, the being a force of Nature instead of a feverish selfish little clod of ailments and grievances, complaining that the world will not devote itself to making you happy."

So live as if you meant it, and become an artist in the same way. This involves a little presumptuous egotism; flow with it. Michelangelo,

Beethoven, Bernhardt, Heifetz, Toscannini, Aeschylus: all great artists have been persons of great dedication and temperament, persons who have sacrificed likability and pleasantness to the drive for perfection that has welled up inside them. If you are determined to "make it" as an actor, you are living life at high stakes anyway. You might as well go all the way with it.

Attitude and capacity for psychological adjustment

How crippling is the comment, "He has a bad attitude!" It keeps talented performers out of work and gets them a place on an informal, rumor-fed blacklist that they may not truly deserve. The slightest whisper, from one associate producer to another, that "we've got enough problems in this show without dealing with *hers!*" is frequently the last exchange before "Thanks very much, dear. We'll be in touch with you if anything comes up."

It may be desirable to be daffy, but it is death to be genuinely crazy—or have producers think you are. Crazy people are hard to contract, do not show up on time, forget their lines and their blocking, annoy other actors, antagonize directors, defy wardrobers, and in general are far more trouble than they are worth. If you are crazy, hide it. If you are not, do not pretend that you are.

But mental health means more than merely being on the near side of psychosis. To be relatively stable, well-balanced, gregarious, and sensitive to the plights of others is a valuable asset. But there are more specific ways in which your attitude can work for you or against you.

Perhaps the worst attitude—the most destructive one—that appears commonly in young actors is the one that says, "I'm waiting to be discovered." This is a complex neurosis, and its effects are virtually fatal. The actor with this attitude is afraid of trying, afraid of looking foolish, afraid of failing. He never contacts agents, never sets up interviews, and never discusses his career or his goals with anyone but close friends. He considers it callous to promote himself, and so dedicates his time to perfecting some small aspect of his craft. Secretly, he hopes that some unknown benefactor will find him in his hidden place of work and sign him to a giant film contract. But he will never take the initiative, because, he says, that would soil his purity.

One must beware of this attitude because it masks itself under seemingly noble forms. Basically it is simple fear and laziness. It is also egotism: the belief that one's own talent is so obvious that it need only be seen once to be instantly appreciated and called into demand. It is also romanticism: no Hollywood movie about the birth of a star has ever shown the aspirant plowing through the yellow pages or passing hours in the waiting rooms of an agent's office: the heroine has been discovered by the producer who visits the little summer stock theatre, or has been the understudy who is called on at the last moment to replace the aging star. The fact is that it takes plain *work* to get work in return, and *you* must go out and do it, because nobody is going to do it for you.

Another attitude that will hurt you if you overplay it is obvious disdain for the role, play, or medium for which you are auditioning. For example, it is not hard to find dozens of people working on a television series who grumble about its lack of artistic integrity. Be careful about jumping on this bandwagon. Most persons working in the theatre, films, or television like what they are doing, at least while they're doing it. At the very least they persuade themselves they like doing it. You may never watch a TV show yourself, but if you are reading for *The Six Million Dollar Man*, it will not help you to take a superior attitude to television or to the premises of the program. The producers, directors, and actors are intelligent, sensitive people. They probably have pride in what they are doing, even if they do not act like it. To mock the show is to mock them, so don't be led into following their self-deprecating remarks. Every director would prefer to cast an actor who will appreciate the role, the play, and the medium.

Discipline is a primary ingredient in the professional actor's attitude. In fact, discipline is usually considered the chief distinction between the amateur and the professional. *Good* colleges, commercial schools, and community theatres insist on it, but these are in a minority. Discipline means that for the entire period between your first call and your dismissal you are concentrating on your tasks as an actor to the exclusion of everything else. It means you are always on time: *not just usually, but always.* (There is absolutely no reason for an actor to be even one minute late to a single audition, rehearsal, or makeup call). It means you are always prompt and ready to do what you are asked, and that all your acting instruments—voice, body, imagination, and intelligence—are at the disposal of the director every moment you are on call.

It is not always easy to see this at work in a professional situation. If you had had the chance to watch, for example, the taping of *Laugh-In*, you would have seen actors lounging around, talking to each other, joking on the set, drinking coffee, dropping lines during takes, and generally exhibiting an air of nonchalance. What you would also have observed, however, was the immediate attention that the director could command, and how within a matter of five seconds 75 people could snap into total concentration and readiness. The nonchalance is necessary relaxation, but it is superficial. These are professionals, conditioned like flight crews to an ever-ready professional alertness. Until you are experienced enough to have one eye always open to the job at hand, concentrate fully on what you are doing. If you do not, you might find yourself still laughing at some joke by the coffeepot while everybody else has suddenly reappeared on the set and the director is calling your name. Angrily.

Artistic temperament can be a drive for perfection and an impatience with inefficiency, or it can mask your inexperience and demonstrate your lack of discipline. It's obviously to your advantage to be easy to work with. Discipline includes a willingness to take direction. No good director will become offended or irritated by genuine questions or discussion about blocking, emphasis, or motivation, but continual complaints such as "It doesn't feel right," particularly when they are obviously meant to cover insecurity, drive directors up walls and may land you out of work. Among professionals, an inability to take direction may become your most talked-about liability, and unless you are sure that your presence in the play or film will draw thousands of paying spectators, you cannot afford that reputation.

The major cliché in director–actor hassles may be mentioned here, although if you have been in any theatre in America you have probably already heard it. That is when the "old school" director (say, George Abbot) tells the "method" actor (say, Marlon Brando) to cross left, and the actor mulls it over and asks, "What's my motivation?" "Your paycheck!" retorts the director. Nothing in today's theatre is that cut and dried, however. The actor–director relationship must be a balanced one, and both parties must genuinely desire to work well together for it to succeed. Obviously, since you are the one who is starting out, you have to do your part and a little bit more, despite possible disagreements.

In short, your attitude should be positive and infectious. You like the part, you like the play, you like the medium, you like the director and his direction, and you want like hell to do it and do it well. Nobody ever really gets offended at an actor who is genuinely eager, unless that eagerness pushes everybody else off the set. No director is offended by an actor who takes it upon himself to read the play being cast beforehand and to prepare an audition for it, or who communicates the genuine feeling that he will work like crazy if he gets the part. While you must never cross over the line by noisily and obsequiously flattering the producers, a certain touch of enthusiasm for the project is bound to be in your favor, and an overall weariness or indifference to it will work against you.

Freedom from entanglements and inhibitions

Freedom is a complex quality and it does not exist in the absolute. Everyone is bound by restraints—practical, financial, social, and mental. Success in the pursuit of an acting career involves minimizing these.

On the first level, an actor must be free to audition for roles and to accept employment when and where offered. The important job offer can come at an awkward time (in the archetypal Hollywood story it always comes as the girl is about to leave on her honeymoon) and can send you to an inconvenient location. You must be free to accept it, however.

On a second level, your commitment to an acting career means a frequent (or at least occasional) slacking-off on other commitments; particularly those to husbands or wives, babies, friends, non-theatre employers, and teachers. Obviously it is better if you can arrange your priority of commitments in such a way that your career plans may proceed unhindered.

Naturally there will be some conflicts of interest here. You are an actor, but you are also a human being in a society, and you have friends, lovers, family, and all sorts of people whose plans and whose feelings will affect yours. After all, there are 8760 hours in a year, and even a fully employed actor will spend 7000 of them away from the set; if you have alienated all your friends just to be at the beck and call of every agent and producer in the business, you are apt to spend a lot of lonely hours by the TV set.

The only thing you can do is to come completely to grips with the nature of the business you are trying to enter and make certain that people who may depend on you are aware of it, too, and sympathetic to your ambitions. They may not be. Many men, for example, have presented the classic ultimatum to would-be fiancees: "I'll marry you if you leave the theatre." And amazingly, many of these men are actors themselves! It is easy to condemn this attitude, but there is one thing you must recognize. If you are starting an acting career, you are not going to be the model wife or husband you learned about in home economics class or even in Masters and Johnson. You will be subject to an ever-changing, unpredictable schedule, you will be on call for location work in Yugoslavia or New Haven while your spouse is taking care of the house and babies, you will be facing the terrific frustration of looking for parts and breaks in an industry where unemployment is routine, and finally, when you start to get work, you will be deeply involved in the emotional crises, love affairs, and strange psychologies of the characters you are given to play. All of this, frankly, can prove incompatible with a happy home life, and the actor or actress must fully prepare himself and his potential spouse for the trials their relationship will inevitably face.

Should an actor get married at all? Well, it is far beyond the scope of this little book to recommend one way or the other, and it is also doubtful that any recommendation here would be very seriously considered anyway. However, it is obvious that marriage *can* become a serious entanglement to a stage or film career if both partners fail to understand what they are getting into. The actor who marries without such understanding either completely frustrates his spouse, and the marriage ends up in ruins, or he frustrates himself, and *he* ends up in ruins. The fact that the acting profession has a ridiculously high divorce rate is one of which you are already aware. For some people it is an either/or situation. In a candid interview, Shelley Winters explains "You see, honey, you've got to really make a choice in life. It's either a good role or a good marriage . . . . I guess I love working more than being married . . . so I gave up this great guy for this great role."* And on it goes: there's no biz like show biz.

Marriage is also a serious entanglement to a young actor if it puts major financial limitations on his career. A young man with a family to support is hardly in a position to spend great portions of his money on photographs, and great portions of his time on unremunerative occupations such as pavement-pounding and waiting-room waiting. If two young actors marry, one may have to get a "regular job" in order to support the other's career, and this can breed resentment.

Ideally a young actor should only marry if he is rich or working, or marrying somebody who is. And he should only marry someone who understands the rigors of the career. Having said this, we rest our case. There are, after all, more than pragmatic considerations in this matter.

There are other entanglements besides marriage, of course. Some are financial, some emotional. You may be unwilling or unable to move around, to work with certain kinds of people, or to play certain kinds of parts. You may object to undressing in front of a camera (or an audience) or performing in a way you find undignified. There is a line you must draw for yourself here, but naturally the lower that line (that is, the fewer your inhibitions) the more "available" you are. Insofar as that line now must be drawn to include or exclude doing nude scenes (which exist in numerous movies) you will have to be prepared to define your views on this if you plan to work in films. There is, however, one "inhibition" that is known as "taste." An actor *must* be inhibited from doing things that are tasteless and unrewarding. Performing in the nude for an Antonioni film and for a one-day stag movie obviously have different values, both as art and as a step in your professional career. A young man or woman who is 100 percent available for a blue film and a $25 fee may find himself or herself unusable for anything *but* that in the future.

Good information and advice

Finally, you need the best current information and advice if you are to pursue a career successfully. This book may be filled with good advice,

* In John Gruen, *Close-Up* (New York: Viking, 1968), p. 48 *ff.*

but it is not enough. You need to know the day-by-day developments in your medium.

Both the theatre and film worlds have their trade journals, which report such developments. In Hollywood these are the *Hollywood Reporter* and *Daily Variety*, published daily during the week and with an annual anniversary issue. In New York they are *Show Business* and *Backstage*, published weekly. In addition, the New York weekly *Variety* provides world-wide coverage of all entertainment media. *Variety* is roughly four times the size of the others. The usefulness of reading the trades is not immediately obvious. Generally they contain information more valuable to producers than to aspiring actors. *Backstage* and *Show Business* (as well as the weekly *Variety*) carry casting columns, but the information is not always current and correct, and important auditions are not always listed. The Hollywood trade papers do not even list casting calls except on very rare occasions; these occur when a studio needs certain types of people badly enough to advertise in the trades. If you live in Los Angeles and subscribe to *Daily Variety*, you may find yourself reading merely who has been cast in what, and who is selling a house in Malibu for $250,000.

On the other hand, it is very much to your advantage to subscribe to the trade papers, or at least to read them from time to time. For one thing, they *are* the most current reports on what is happening in your business. Even if the information is not particularly relevant to your immediate interest (getting work), it will give you a basic understanding of what is going on. It will let you know what is on the minds of agents, producers, and casting directors, and give you a vocabulary of names, places, and shows being done in your area. Both papers regularly list the names of agents, casting directors, and people you should try to know, and you can at least start to become familiar with who they are in case you meet them. Furthermore, reading the papers gives you a vicarious sense of participation in the business even if you have not really started out, and it will help you overcome your naturally alien feelings.

Where else do you get information? Talk to people. Actors love to talk about their business—some of them talk about almost nothing else. Acting schools are good places to begin, and theatre bars, particularly in New York, another. Or simply go to a lot of shows—the off-off-Broadway workshops in New York or Los Angeles. Even if you don't know a soul in the production, hang around after the curtain call and wander backstage. If there were actors whose performances you liked, congratulate them (an always-effective calling card) and introduce yourself.

At worst you will engage in an agreeable little conversation. At best you will strike up a true and valuable friendship (some of the very best have begun in precisely this manner). And friends, of course, are a very fine source of information, perhaps the best there is. With friends in the trade you can get a feeling for the intangibles which control this emotional and frequently mystical business. You can sense out the tips, the hunches, the possibilities and the probabilities which determine so much of the day-to-day course of the trade's events. You can get a sense of the feelings of the people in charge—and the people under them. But beware of being overly influenced by any single person's likes, dislikes, neuroses, or phobias. Gradually you will gain a working knowledge of what casting possibilities are hot, which agents are really working for which actors, which producers are open to what kinds of suggestions, and in general what your competition is likely to be.

There are theatre schools that specialize in teaching you "how to audition" and "how to get a job," as well as "how to act." They may be useful. There are also public lectures on these subjects from time to time; they are usually advertised in trade magazines. Of course, there are always a lot of people willing to take your money in return for "inside" tips and suggestions. With these people you begin to reach the point of diminishing returns, however. No matter how much you may read or hear about the subject of "making it" in acting, nothing begins to approach the knowledge you get by working toward success yourself. The best way to learn the business is to get started, to participate. The suggestions in the rest of the book will indicate some ways to do it. Once you get your start, you can leave this book behind. You will be finding information much more specifically applicable to your needs.

Luck

Luck is placed last on this list, simply because there is nothing you can do to get it. Luck is a factor that can outweigh most of the rest, and there is nothing to do about it but groan.

In the British theatre, acting success can be achieved merely by ascending a very well-defined ladder. If you are good enough (as proved by audition) to gain admission to the Royal Academy of Dramatic Art (or any of the top six drama schools in London), and good enough to stay in through graduation, you are virtually assured employment at one of the many regional repertory companies in the British Isles. From there it is simply a matter of perfecting your craft, and "working up" to one of the prestigious companies, the National Theatre and the Royal Shakespeare Company being at the top of the heap. If you become a leading performer at one of the leading companies, you will most probably be offered film roles. British actors tend to be a lot less neurotic than their American counterparts, since the steps to a career are so clearly laid out.

In America luck is much more important, particularly in film acting. Witness Shelly Duvall, the young starlet of *Brewster McCloud, McCabe and Mrs. Miller,* and *Thieves Like Us.* Miss Duvall, at the time she was cast in *Brewster,* had never studied acting, had never seen a play, and generally disdained theatre people as "weird." She was a suburban housewife living in Houston, Texas, and she was "discovered" while selling her husband's paintings to people who turned out to be MGM producers. The dream of "discovery" lies deep in the heart of every aspiring performer, but it comes almost as often to those who do not work for it as to those who do. Shirley MacLaine was "discovered" when she was called upon to substitute for Carol Haney in the Broadway musical, *Pajama Game.* Hal Wallis was in the audience, and but for that occurrence, Miss MacLaine might still be hoofing on 45th Street. It also turned out that MacLaine was planning to resign from the show the very night that Haney turned her ankle. But what do *you* do about luck? You don't go to Houston to sell oil paintings; that's for sure. You will have to find your own.

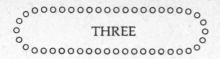

What do you do now?

Well, we now assume that you are convinced you have talent, and are prepared to make a career. You are going to look for work, so what do you do now?

Your medium

The three theatrical media are stage, film, and broadcasting (which for all practical purposes means television). Allied media in which you may find employment are variety and nightclub work and modeling, but we shall limit our concern to the three acting media. These are divided into subgroups. Included in professional stage work are Broadway and off-Broadway shows, summer stock and regional repertory companies, outdoor theatres, dinner theatres, industrial productions, and guest-artist stints at drama schools and universities. Included in film are feature films and documentaries. In television there are filmed and taped specials, series shows, commercials, and live announcing positions. Since television makes great use of filmed programming, the two media are virtually inseparable from the actor's point of view, and no real choice need be made between them at the early stages of a career. Your major decision, then, is between stage and camera work.

You should first seek advice from your teachers and valued critic/ friends on the medium that best suits you. In weighing the alternatives open to you, you should take the following points into consideration.

Stage work demands great versatility and projection. Stage actors are called upon to do a wide variety of roles, frequently before a thousand or more people at one sitting. A strong, penetrating voice capable of great subtlety is an absolute necessity. You should have a face that projects emotion without mugging, a body that moves well, and a personality that without pushing carries well beyond the footlights. Similarly, you should have a command of verse-speaking and classical acting styles, because most stage careers begin in theatres that produce classical plays. Strong talents in the areas of music and dance are valuable to the stage actor, though not absolutely necessary. Above all, the stage actor needs the great intangibles; talent, presence, and timing. He must be able to enunciate the subtlest nuances clearly to huge audiences without looking as if he were reading from a speech textbook, and he must convey the sense of a vibrant personality whether he is playing hero, villain, or village idiot.

If your talents lie, on the other hand, in the area of extremely naturalistic performing, a film or television career is probably more suitable. Acting before a camera ruthlessly shows up all but the most honest of performers. It virtually obviates the need for projection, since the camera and microphone can be placed inches away. It is frequently said that the film actor is the pawn of the director, cameraman, editor, and sound mixer. "The cameraman usurps the actor's physical composition, the sound mixer his intonation, and the editor his timing," according to one highly successful stage and film actor. Thus, for the camera actor it is personality, looks, "quality," and honesty that become premium qualifications.

In general a person's looks count less for him in live theatre than in camera theatre, mainly because makeup can do much more at 50 feet than in a larger-than-life film close-up. Many persons who are genuinely plain have had brilliant stage careers but have found it impossible to get work in Hollywood. By contrast, a person who is astonishingly beautiful or interesting in a unique way can begin to get film work almost on that basis alone.

Your home base

One more element to consider is where you want to live. As an actor you really have only three choices: you can live in New York, you can live in Los Angeles-Hollywood, or you can live in the spiderweb of the LORT-CORST-COST-ADTI-MTA circuits. These choices involve different kinds of theatrical activity and different life styles and business procedures for you.

The LORT-CORST-COST-ADTI-MTA circuits: regional theatre

The regional theatre market has had, over the past years, numerous ups and downs, but it currently seems to be having something of an up, particularly in the nonprofit LORT sector, and in the burgeoning dinner theatre phenomenon. Regional theatres serve their immediate communities, but are linked into loose alliances with acronymic titles.

LORT is the League of Resident Theatres, which are nonprofit professional theatres in the major American cities: The Arena Stage in Washington, DC, The Guthrie Theatre in Minneapolis, the American Conservatory Theatre in San Francisco, the Long Wharf in New Haven, and so forth. These theatres produce independent work of exceptionally high quality. Many of them have federal grants to pursue experimental work and talent development; some have affiliations with universities, and others have conservatories of their own. In addition to their stage work, many LORT theatres have been invited to have their productions taped for national Public Broadcasting System (PBS) telecasting. Clearly, for an actor, the LORT circuit is the plum of regional theatre activities. The work of these theatres is regularly reviewed in trade papers, scholarly journals, and occasionally *The New York Times*, and an outstanding paperback has been issued by the Theatre Communications Group detailing the workings of all 30-odd LORT theatres, as well as another 60 or so nonprofit but professional (or close-to-professional) theatre operations.*

*Theatre Profiles, Volume 1, 1973. Theatre Communications Group, Inc., 355 Lexington Avenue, New York, NY 10017. $4.00. Future editions are expected.

CORST, the Council of Resident Stock Theatres, and COST, the Council of Stock Theatres, are associations of commercial theatres that present plays for stock runs, usually one or more weeks, and usually in the summer only, although some go year-round. CORST theatres must have a resident company of at least seven Equity members; many of them have apprentice programs and offer some possibilities for local actors (called "local jobbers") as well. COST theatres need have no stable company, and in fact frequently produce prepackaged shows that simply bus from one COST theatre to another each week. Additionally there are theatres allied with MTA (Musical Theatre Association) and ACMT (Association of Civic Musical Theatres), which produce musical theatre extravaganzas, principally in the middle west, and again mainly in the summertime.

The ADTI is the American Dinner Theatre Institute, and it represents only a fraction of the professional dinner theatres, which have grown dramatically in the past few years, now numbering in the hundreds. Dinner theatre productions tend toward light comedies and musicals; they are combined not only with pre-theatre dinners, but occasionally post-theatre dancing and merriment, and comprise a fairly all-encompassing entertainment medium. Some dinner theatres are beginning to offer apprentice programs, and apprentices who elect to serve as waiters and waitresses can make up to $200 per week while training. Dinner theatres also offer the occasional opportunity of year-round employment, which is a godsend to most actors; conversely the dinner theatre credit is not always a particularly helpful stepping stone to "eatless" ventures. But this may change. Dinner theatres are on the move—not only in the provinces, but in major metropolitan markets—and the "Ham with Hamlet" operation might well dominate the stage world of future decades.

Outdoor Drama Festivals are a diverse category of theatre production companies that span the range from Equity operations like the New York and Oregon Shakespeare Festivals to the nonpaying and lowpaying enterprises in the South and Southeast. The principal outdoor theatres, which are loosely associated in an Institute of Outdoor Drama headquartered at the University of North Carolina, are listed in the Appendix to this book (as are the principal LORT theatres and ADTI theatres).

The regional theatre offers a certain amount of work, an opportunity to break into that work, and the possibility of intermediate engagement via apprenticeships and journeyman contracts—a possibility that is unknown in New York or Los Angeles. The principal theatres in each category operate under one of nearly a dozen different Equity contracts, and an Equity card may eventually be gained in any one of them, giving you the opportunity to join the sister unions (SAG and AFTRA) merely by paying the initiation fee. And in the LORT theatres, and even occasionally in one of the others, you may find the opportunity for national exposure in highly significant and artistic work. However, there is very little vertical mobility among these various circuits of the acting industries, and credits from dinner theatres do not easily translate to opportunities in LORT; similarly LORT credits do not make an immediate impression on Broadway or the Hollywood studios. Some people are quite happy with this, and are able to lead their entire careers in regional theatre, finding there a high degree of artistic fulfillment and social satisfaction. Others eventually get frustrated. Rene Auberjonois, a superb regional actor who "went on" to Broadway and Hollywood success, gives his reasons for leaving LORT: "I am convinced that most actors involved in regional theatre are schizophrenics in the sense that they cannot reconcile the feeling that they should be fighting the fight of commercial theatre with the feeling that they are chosen members of some great and holy theatrical crusade. This dilemma gives rise to a working climate which could be compared to a monastery filled with self-consciously zealous monks suppressing the desire to ravage the neighboring village."* It is evident that some of this schizophrenia is felt, if not to the same degree, by virtually everybody in the regional theatre.

Auditioning for regional theatres

Most of the casting for regional theatres of all types is done in New York, or in the Equity offices of Chicago, Los Angeles, San Francisco, or Toronto. This is true for the LORT theatres as well as the more directly commercial ones. However, the great majority of theatres,

* "The Regional Theatre: Four Views" *The Drama Review*, Vol. 13, No. 1 (Fall 1968).

other than those that simply present prepackaged productions, do at least a little casting at home. Some of this, quite frankly, is for a public relations effect: it gives the local community a sense of participation in the theatre, and helps to generate good will—and audiences. Thus most of the LORT companies have fairly regular open-call auditions for local actors and aspirants. Some hold these as often as every month (as does, for example, the Center Theatre Group in Los Angeles), some once a season. The Virginia Museum Theatre (Richmond) is fairly typical; its producing director, Keith Fowler, writes:

> Locally, we see anyone who wants to come to audition, Equity or non-Equity. We hold open calls once in the fall (the best time, because we're really looking for actors then) and once in the spring (not such a good time, because we're thinking more of relieving the congestion in the "waiting line" than casting our winter season). We ask each person to prepare (memorize) two contrasting selections of about two minutes each, and to send in or bring with them an 8 x 10 and a résumé. It's surprising how many non-Equity people don't bring the photo—it's impossible to remember an actor without the picture.

Although a company's open calls are not advertised in the newspapers, a letter of inquiry or a telephone call will probably get you the required information about time and place. The same is true for dinner theatres. Marvin Poons, Executive Secretary of the ADTI, writes:

> The only effective method of securing employment in dinner theatres currently is to write to each theatre in which you are interested and request an audition. From my experience, if a young actor is willing to make the trip, he will be given a courteous reception and an unhurried audition.

These are not promises, but probabilities.

So write or call any theatre that strikes your fancy, and that you are willing to travel to, and try to arrange for an appointment, or an open-call audition. Be prepared with two photos and résumés (one to send ahead, one to have ready to give them if they've mislaid the first), and be prepared to write again—and again—if your original letter goes unanswered. Most LORT theatres receive between 400 and 1000 new résumés and applications *per week* during their casting seasons, and few of these companies have the facilities and staff to process this enormous correspondence with complete accuracy. Make the most out of any reply you do get.

As to your chances of gaining employment as a non-Equity local "jobber" with a LORT company, they are small but not absolutely zero. Again, the VMT's Mr. Fowler:

> The best chance a non-Equity person has for getting a role from us is to be, first of all, an outstanding actor, and secondly a local resident. Then we know he will be easily available and won't need much money to live on. The odds against the auditioning actor are of course incredibly high. We see a good many fine actors, both Equity and non-Equity. We have a very good selection to choose from; it's a buyers' market. What isn't widely known is that we often see fresh faces that we want very much to give jobs to. I can think of three actors right now that I would dearly love to work with. Sometimes the roles aren't right for these people though, and you can't use them, much as you'd like to. More often, you can think of roles, but you already have actors who are just as good and who are already your friends and artistic companions, and you're certainly not going to bump them out of their jobs to make room for the new face. We have to remember that auditioning is a process for discovering a few new actors for your company, not for casting all your roles. Most roles are cast with actors who are already hard-working members of your ensemble.

So understand this picture, and try to fit yourself into it in one way or another.

Unified auditions

If you are a college senior or recent graduate, you will have a marvelous opportunity to contract with a LORT theatre by attending the Chicago auditions sponsored by the Theatre Communications Group (TCG) previously mentioned. TCG is an autonomous, nonprofit organization operated with funds from the Ford Foundation; it seeks to coordinate the activities (particularly casting) of the LORT theatres. Each fall TCG writes to the drama department heads at all U.S. colleges. These department heads (usually in consultation with their faculties) nominate about 500 students, who must be seniors or graduates from the past year. These students audition at regional centers before TCG representatives in January. The regional centers are Los Angeles, New York, San Francisco, Seattle, Chicago, St. Louis, Austin, Cincinnati, Washington, Detroit, Atlanta, and Boston. From these regional quali-fying auditions about 80 candidates are invited to final auditions in Chicago. These are held in March, and to them come the artistic directors and company managers of virtually all the LORT companies. According to TCG officials, about half of the auditioners are offered "immediate employment," (beginning the following September). Some of these offers of employment involve non-Equity apprenticeships. The apprentice is offered a small salary, a chance to act, and the eventual possibility of earning an Equity card. Sometimes the offers are for journeyman positions, which are reduced-rate Equity jobs, and not infrequently the actor may be offered a full Equity contract. Obviously the Chicago auditions are a superb opportunity, and any actor with stage ambitions should do his best to get into them, and to do as well as he can in them. Later in this chapter we shall discuss the auditions themselves, and how to prepare for them.

Unfortunately you cannot get to the Chicago auditions without first qualifying in the regional auditions, and you cannot get into the qualification round without a nomination from the head of your drama department. If your department does not nominate you, there is nothing you can do via TCG, and you should not try. Every year students not nominated show up in Chicago hoping to get an audition squeezed in because of a no-show. It never happens. "Absolutely and unequivocally not," say the directors of TCG. But remember, if you are not nominated by your department upon graduation, you still have two years of eligibility, and even though you may not apply directly for a nomination, it would not be considered unwise or presumptuous, in most cases, to make your interest in a nomination known to the proper people.

Although the Chicago TCG auditions are the best single opportunity for breaking into regional theatre, there are two other unified auditions of some importance. The University Resident Theatre Association (URTA) is "an organization of professionally oriented college and university theatres," and URTA holds annual auditions in various U.S. locations during the year. URTA has 35 members, including the Asolo Theatre (Florida), the Utah Shakespeare Festival, the Harvard Summer

School Repertory Theatre, The Globe of the Great Southwest, and several others, and many of these cast from the URTA auditions, which placed 200 actors in paying positions during 1973. It should be stressed that the bulk of the URTA offerings are graduate assistantships at universities, and are not directly in line with Equity performing situations, but they are paid acting opportunities, and should be considered by any college graduate as a possibility. An URTA candidate, like a TCG candidate, must be recommended by the chairman of his or her department with the approval of staff colleagues, but you can start the ball rolling by an inquiry to URTA at its national headquarters at Columbia University, New York, NY 10027. Also, the Institute of Outdoor Drama (University of North Carolina, Chapel Hill, NC 26514) runs a unified audition in the spring for a large number of outdoor summer theatricals, and can provide information about other unified auditions held from time to time on this circuit.

New York and Hollywood

If you are not auditioning in Chicago and are not headed for a LORT-CORST-COST-ADTI general audition, or are not interested in the regional scene to begin with, you will be headed for New York or Hollywood. Nowhere else, really. Virtually all live professional theatre is cast in New York—even LORT productions are generally cast there. TCG, for example, has audition facilities for the year-round use of LORT directors who come to town for that purpose. Summer stock casts in New York, as do industrial shows, dinner shows, and touring shows. Even Los Angeles producers of live theatre do some of their casting in New York (much to the dismay and fury of local actors). Conversely, most film features, all filmed network television, and much live TV are cast in Hollywood, and many of the programs and films are made there, too. If you are a stage actor, you should go to New York. If camera is your medium, go West. Go, in any case, where your share of the action is likely to be.

As cities, New York and Hollywood are as unalike as Paris and Peking. New York is a filthy town which is either loved or hated by everyone who comes in contact with it. The old chestnut, "New York's a great place to visit, but I wouldn't want to live there," has never before been so well earned. "Fun City" is beset with urban ills that make most of those anywhere else seem, in scale, as bothersome as a few broken street lights. The city is grimy; overpriced; over-robbed; over-mugged; and riddled with dope addiction, racial and religious chaos, broken-down transportation, bitter people, a bad climate, and a general feeling of futility. Despite all this there are those who love New York, those to whom the prospect of crossing over the Hudson River into the city sends chills up and down the spine. New York for all its faults, is at the very pulse of America, and there is a feeling about living in the midst of that power that makes anywhere else seem "hick."

Los Angeles is blessed with a fairer climate but cursed with a miserably polluted atmosphere, nonexistent public transportation, a crazy city layout that has virtually no downtown area, lethargic people, a generally anti-cultural atmosphere, and an unstable populace that moves in and out at a rate of nearly 5000 people a week. There is almost nothing exciting about Los Angeles itself; there are virtually no public places where actors congregate without an invitation, and exclusivity imposes a special kind of remoteness that the young actor may never find his way out of. You can become part of the New York "scene" in a matter of weeks, but you may live in Los Angeles for years without even finding a Hollywood equivalent to it. Even telephoning someone across town results in a toll charge, and getting to his house without your own car takes half a day. These factors themselves may help you make up your mind. After all, it is not just your career, it is your whole life that is up for grabs; and you ought to decide what kinds of environmental problems you are best at facing.

Jumping media

Actors are frequently advised to go to New York to build up credits before coming to Hollywood. This implies a great interchange between media and a certain ease in jumping from one to the other. It is certainly true that among the finest new male film actors are a number who began their careers in live theatre in New York; these are Stacy Keach, Robert Duvall, Al Pacino, Frank Langella, Dustin Hoffman, Alan Arkin, and others like them. Yet these men had reached virtually "star" status in New York (at least off-Broadway) before the film industry began to notice them. Few women make the jump at all. Colleen Dewhurst, a superb New York actress with credits and awards three blocks long, admits, when asked why she has done only two small film roles in her career, "It's because nobody's asked me." And as the sometime wife of George C. Scott, she does not lack contacts.

The truth is that it is very difficult to transfer credits from New York to Hollywood as you would, for example, from one graduate school to another. Minor credits in one town are almost worthless as stepping stones in the other; they can even be a hindrance among Hollywood producers highly suspicious of "arty" off-Broadway and Broadway performers. New York actors come to Hollywood and moan, "They've never heard of me!" even though they may have major, man-on-the-street reputations back home. "Off-Broadway auditions for Broadway, which auditions for Hollywood," says veteran multimedia performer James Coco, but Coco's own career attests that Hollywood only pays attention to those who first rise to the top in the East.

Part of the difficulty in jumping from one medium to another is that few actors are equally adept at both. The different qualities mentioned earlier (projection versus intimacy) apply not just at the beginning of an actor's career, but all the way through. Most actors, truthfully, are not universally accomplished; producers have frequently despaired after casting a film star in a stage lead or vice versa. Another difficulty is simply the ignorance most Hollywood directors and producers have of New York theatre. New York is, after all, 2500 miles distant, and film people on a trip East aren't eager to probe Greenwich Village for discoveries. Frank Langella, for example, had won numerous off-Broadway awards, had played several seasons of summer stock, and had performed a leading role at New York's Lincoln Center long before he was tapped for his first film role. The same is true of virtually everyone who has successfully jumped from the stage to the screen.

So it is folly to assume, as many do, that the young actor can spend a couple of years in New York to "get exposure" and then head for Hollywood with credits under his arm. He will have only a suitcase under his arm, and he will have to start all over. The best suggestion we can make is to decide which medium you will be best at, now, next year, and three years from now, and head for the proper geographical center.

Establishing yourself

You have moved, then, to your new city. The first thing you must do is to *establish* yourself. Obviously you need a place to stay. If you are going to New York, and you have not been there before, prepare yourself: you will not believe what you are asked to pay for the dingiest apartment or hotel room imaginable. If possible, move in with a friend and give yourself a couple of weeks to look for a rent-controlled apartment in a decent area; better yet, move to New York with a friend or two and share a place and the rent among you. Bring enough money to pay two months' rent in advance plus a deposit, plus a few hundred dollars in reserve. If you head for Los Angeles, you can expect to find a more reasonably priced place to stay. What is more, it will be cleaner and nicer to come home to; the limitation there is you absolutely must have a car in good running condition, which eats up whatever you may save on rent.

Once you are settled, you can get to work. There will be many things you need. There is no particular order in which you should get them, but you should get them fast. These are:

A dependable source of income

A telephone and a telephone service

Pictures of yourself

A résumé of your training and experience

Colleagues

Up-to-date information

An agent

A dependable source of income

Obviously you need this. You cannot pay your bills, eat, dress, or go out into the world without money. Moreover, you cannot afford to scrimp on professional expenses like photographs and classes. Perhaps you have regular income from home, or from your working husband, or from an indulgent lover. That is magnificent and you need not worry so long as your source continues to take care of you, though generally something is expected in return. If you are not so lucky, you will have to get a job, and preferably one with flexible hours that pays well. In Hollywood, since most work and interviews are done in the daytime, an evening job (say, as a waiter or waitress) is ideal. In New York the same is true until you start to perform or work at night in off-off-Broadway. Many actors work graveyard shifts in New York to be available during all "normal" hours. The back pages of trade journals frequently advertise part-time jobs particularly suitable to the personalities and strange schedules of aspiring actors.

One agent recommends that anyone coming to New York or Hollywood first prepare himself or herself with a salable skill, and he goes on to suggest office skills—stenography and typing—as ideal ones. Why? Financial solvency is vitally important. It may take three to five years before you even know *if* you're ever going to make money in sufficient quantities to live, and in bad times unskilled odd jobs are scarcer than acting jobs. At least a secretary works and eats, and if you land the right kind of job in a theatre-related area, you start to get contacts while you work. There are many young men and women (male secretaries are now commonplace in Hollywood and becoming so in New York) who have started in the office and ended up on stage. Anything—hairdressing, bartending, housepainting—is better in the long run than making porny films for hack photographers on Sunset Boulevard.

How much money will you need? In these inflationary times there is no sure way of knowing, but a young actor of our acquaintance wrote recently that the minimum figure on which an actor can expect to pursue a career in New York is $125 a week. "I mean you just have to have that, you just *have* to," he says. This actor came to New York with a nest egg of a few hundred dollars, "all but a nickel" of which was put down as advance rent on what turned out to be a nonexistent apartment. So bring some money, make some money, and take care of your money—and don't be ashamed of it. If you collect unemployment checks, or money from home, pretend, as our here-cited friend did, that the envelopes say "National Foundation for the Arts" on them.

A telephone and telephone service

These are both musts. You must be reachable to get any work at all, and nobody in New York or Los Angeles relies on the mail service for this. A telephone will cost you anywhere from $8.00 to $12.00 a month (plus long-distance charges) and is a virtual necessity. There will be times when you do not want to stay home and wait for it to ring, so you need a telephone service, too. The service either answers your phone for you when you are out (via an electronic hookup), or takes messages for you at another number when you cannot be reached at yours. The first service is apt to cost about $25 a month, and while it is preferable due to its simplicity (you need only give out one number to agents and producers), the "if no answer" service is much cheaper (as low as $5 monthly) and just as effective. In either case you soon get in the habit of calling your service whenever you get home to see if there are any messages for you, and you face the discouragement of hearing the bright voice on the other end gaily declare, "No messages today!" or "All clear!" If you pale at the thought of continually calling your service and getting the inevitably discouraging results, or if you have a good sum of money to invest in a long-term saving, you might buy a recording device which attaches to your telephone and answers it for you, playing your own recorded voice to your callers and recording their message for your eventual playback when you return. This device costs anywhere from $150 up, and more expensive versions can be programmed in such a way that you can call your own phone from wherever you happen to be and listen to messages that have come in since you left; it is every bit as good as a personal answering service and less expensive over a couple of years.

Photographs

These, as we have mentioned, are your calling cards. No actor can be without photographs, which are in two basic forms:

Photographs for distribution. These are mass produced and, together with your résumé, are given out to anybody who seems to have a professional reason for wanting them.

Photographs in your "book," which you carry around to interviews and auditions and show to interested directors and producers.

Of course you need both, but they can be acquired at the same time. The standard procedure is for the actor to go to a photographer and have a set of photos made; you then select one or two to mass-duplicate, and others to go in your book. The duplications are rarely made by the photographer (who, unless he specializes in mass printing, will charge up to $2.00 apiece for them). Instead, you send them to one of the quantity reproduction laboratories in New York or Los Angeles that print them for as little as 11¢ or 12¢ apiece. You can find excellent quantity reproduction labs listed in the yellow pages of both cities; call them for current prices.

Finding a photographer and selecting the kind of photographs you will need, however, is a much more complex process. There is great disagreement over what is desirable in the way of photographs, and you will probably experiment many times before you land a successful portfolio of photos. All should be on 8 x 10 glossy stock. Here are the variables:

Formats: Single head shot
Composite head shots
Composite head shots plus abbreviated résumé
Body shots
Composite of head and body shots

Style: Studio-posed
Candid

Film: 35mm
2¼ in., or 120
View camera (5 x 7, 4 x 5, or 8 x 10)

Naturally, with thousands of actors and thousands of photographers all aiming at some sort of originality, there are bound to be countless variations on the above alternatives, and some undoubtedly succeed.

The composite photograph is a laboratory print that combines two or more shots of you into a single 8 x 10 photo. Three or four poses are common, but some composites have five, six, or seven shots crammed into the 80 square inches. The idea of a composite is to show the various expressions, attitudes, and characteristics of your face and your personality. Frequently each separate shot is in a different costume, and perhaps also a different makeup. One shot is often considerably larger than the others, and becomes your "basic" look, with the other shots supporting it by showing "what else you can look like." A good composite must be done with great precision in the laboratory, so that light levels in the various shots balance each other, the lines separating the prints are straight and even, and the overall composition is effective. Often the actor's name, agent, and phone number can be printed right on the composite and his résumé printed on the back, though this is expensive.

Most producers, however (particularly in theatre and film work, as opposed to commercials), prefer the straight, full, 8 x 10 head shot. This is universally true in Hollywood, and about 70 percent true in New York. Why? The head shot makes a bold, single impression. The Hollywood casting director does not want to hire you for four roles, but just for one. The composite dilutes your look. Surprisingly, this also seems to be true for repertory company casting directors, who will simply assume that you can change under makeup. The principal goal of your photographs should be to show you *as you are*. That which is beautiful, dramatic, sensitive, virile, or interesting in your appearance should appear to be coming from you rather than from some darkroom magician.

The same considerations apply to the style and format of your pictures. You should know enough of the nature of photography to make an intelligent choice here.

Studio-posed photographs are generally made with a studio or view camera. It is called a view camera because the photographer can preview his exact photograph (upside down) on a ground glass screen behind the camera. The view camera uses large film: usually 4 x 5 and sometimes as large as 8 x 10. This gives him two advantages: first he can make all sorts of corrections on his negative, such as airbrushing away facial blemishes and compensating for weak features in your bone structure. Secondly, his print will be enlarged at most only four times its negative size, so that the quality (resolution, or sharpness) will be superior, and the lighting and shading effects, as well as your skin tone, can be subtle. Also, the studio conditions allow him to light the subject (you) effectively and with fine attention to detail. The photographic portraits by Karsh of Ottawa, for example, use this process and are considered masterpieces.

On the other hand, the studio and its camera impose huge limitations. Their very photographic superiority bespeaks a kind of staleness, a 1950's phoniness. Just as films are now made almost entirely on location instead of on a sound stage, most contemporary photographic portraiture is done outdoors under "natural light" conditions, and for the same reasons. Outdoor candid photography conveys a vitality that does not come across in posed studio photographs, no matter how good. Thirty-five millimeter film is far less expensive than the larger variety, and a photographer can take thirty-six different candid shots with the same amount of film it takes for *one* 8 x 10 view camera exposure. Since the 35-mm camera is light and small, a photographer and subject can roam freely and easily in many locations, shooting quickly and easily without posing at all, and come home with 500 negatives to choose from. The limitation of this form of photography, of course, is that the negative must be enlarged nearly 40 times to make an 8 x 10 print (even more if the negative is "cropped"—that is, if only a fraction of it is actually used), and the print quality tends to be grainy and without delicate shadings. For a dramatic and exciting photograph, however, this is not a limitation. The very graininess, according to many producers (and even photographers) is an asset (it gives a picture liveliness and a sense of movement) and the natural, unretouched look gives a photo charm and a sense of authenticity. Besides, motion picture films themselves are made on 35-mm stock, so there is little sense in previewing yourself in the larger film when they are looking for you in the smaller.

A very popular compromise in film size is the "120," which is used in twin-lens-reflex cameras like the Rolleiflex, or the fine Swedish single-lens reflex, the Hasselblad. This photography uses a negative that is 2¼ inches square and produces a finer print than the 35 mm, with less graininess and more subtlety. It costs a few cents more per shot. The 2¼ inch camera is only a little larger than the 35 mm and has no significant limitations.

How much should a beginning portfolio cost? There are professional photographers in New York and Los Angeles who specialize in photographing actors. Their services run anywhere from $50 to $500 and more for a session, which can vary from a single studio sitting to an all-day romp with camera in Central Park. Be sure of what you are getting.

What you need, basically, are about five to ten good shots of yourself. They should look like you do *at your best*. They should mainly be head shots and head-and-shoulder shots, though you can have one from the waist up if you wish. (*No* cheesecakes, unless you are auditioning for a Las Vegas strip show.) The photographer will take his shots and in a day or so show you proof sheets from which to make your selections. He will then print the eight or ten you select. His fee for this will vary enormously, depending on his market value; you can pay as little as $50 for this, but you will probably pay more for a good photographer. If you pay more than $125, you should have evidence that he is one of the very best, because that fee is high. You then take the best shot and have a hundred copies made for about $15. The copies should be virtually as good as the original, or you can have them redone.

Different photographers have different setups, of course, and may offer to sell their prints in other combinations. Some will include the mass-produced 100 copies in their price (usually they will send them to the same place you would and add twice the cost). Others charge a flat rate for the session and two final prints, and additional fees for everything else, including the making of composites. Others simply charge a sitting fee and a per print charge beyond that; this is surely the fairest way.

Frequently the photographer will offer other services as well. Some have a means of offset-printing your photograph onto regular bond paper; they can then print your résumé on the back. Composites are a standard photographic process, and your photographer will advise you on how to make up a composite from your individual proofs, if you desire one. In general the photographer will have his own ideas on how you should be photographed and what you should have; he will also be happy to tell you which shots *he* prefers and which ones producers are likely to prefer. The trouble is that he is not really apt to know more than you do; it is simply a good business practice to act as if he did. Remember, *he* is not going for work, *you* are. His income comes from taking pictures, not acting in plays or movies. Still, his reputation comes from the actors he has photographed who have gone on to successful careers, and his advice should be listened to with attention.

There is nothing to prevent you and a friend from getting together and taking your own photographs, and though the professionals will gripe at our saying this, there's no great mystique in photography that time and care cannot master. Simply go to a camera store and rent for a day or two a good 35-mm single-lens-reflex camera with a through-the-lens light meter and buy half a dozen rolls of Tri-X film. The camera shop owner will be happy to explain the camera's operation, and you and your friend can go out and shoot each other all day long. Using the camera's meter correctly will give you the right exposure. Remember, though, to recheck the exposure and focus for every shot. To avoid the pitfalls that make most amateurish snapshots just that—amateurish snapshots—keep in mind (and ask your friend to keep in mind) these basic rules:

1. Get in *close*. Remember those dramatic head shots and head-and-shoulder shots you've seen, and move in to your subject until that's what you see in the viewfinder. Let the face fill at least half and preferably up to two-thirds of the frame.

2. Hold the camera so that the framed image is bigger vertically than horizontally. You don't have to do this every time, but you will probably get most of your best-composed shots this way.

3. Avoid complicated backgrounds, especially those that are cluttered or busy or that contain bold contrasts or heavy straight lines. Don't frame the shot so that a tree appears to be growing out of the top of your subject's head.

4. Every 35-mm single-lens-reflex camera has a depth-of-field preview button or lever. Have the dealer show you where it is and how to use it. Set it (do this before you start shooting) in the preview position, then set the diaphragm (lens opening) ring to get as much as possible of the background *out of focus*. Release the preview button and continue. Always, of course, keep your subject *in* focus.

5. Forget what you were told long ago about needing bright sun behind you while taking pictures. That rule is what caused all those awful snapshots of squinting faces with chalky highlights and black shadows. If possible, shoot on a bright *cloudy* day or in the shade. If you shoot in bright sunlight, keep the sun at the subject's side or back, and avoid patches of bright sunlight on part of the subject's face.

6. Keep the subject's face and body in a place roughly parallel to the plane of the camera back. Having any part of the subject much

closer to the camera than the rest of her or him will produce a picture in which that part of the person looks like a grotesquely overgrown deformity.

7. Relax the subject. Talk, joke, distract him. Have him bob his head and shoot him as he comes up. Give him things to say and do, then stop him with a word and shoot. Or shoot him without stopping him. Take a variety of poses: smiles, laughs (genuine!), glares, thoughtful reflections, full-face stares, angled gazes, profiles. You can pick the best later. Avoid "arty" shadowy photos; they only make the agent or director wonder what is being concealed—and why.

8. Enjoy yourself. The advantages of doing photographs yourself is that you can spend more time just horsing around and capturing some jolly, spontaneous moods. These are quite likely to result in fine photos. You can mix in mood shots, but be prepared not to like them when you see them developed later.

You will come home with about 100 shots of each of you, and some of them are bound to be good ones. Have the film developed and printed on contact sheets by the camera store, and then have the best negatives enlarged. For a dollar or two extra (and maybe for free, if you are now a good friend of the camera shop owner) you can have the choicest negatives "custom printed" and they will be "cropped" (shaped) and printed with special care. On the West Coast the approximate cost of all this, for the two of you, would be as follows:

Camera rental, 1 day	$ 5
Film (six 36-exposure cartridges)	9
Developing	6
Contact sheets	12
10 prints (8 x 10 glossy)	30
Total	$62

This comes out to a little more than $30 apiece, and if you can find a friend with a darkroom, you can probably shave that figure by half. If you have taken some good shots, you have not only saved money, you may get ideas about opening up a little source of side income for yourself. If, on the other hand, the contact sheets look terrible, you don't have to have them printed, and you have not lost much money.

Résumés

The actor's résumé is a listing of the parts he has played (and where) on a single mimeographed sheet, together with such basic information as his name, height, hair color, eye color, weight, age range, and telephone number (or agent's telephone number), plus any further information that might be helpful in getting work. The sheet is mimeographed or otherwise duplicated, and attached to the photograph. Some photographers can do this as part of the printing process, but there is nothing wrong with simply stapling a résumé to the back of a photo. No actor ever got hired because of an expensive printing job on his photo-résumé and none has ever lost a part because his credits were mimeographed and not offset. Neatness is important; opulence is not.

What information should you list? As to your physical characteristics, be realistic. If you are a girl and weigh in at 150, you'd better say so or they will be mad when you show up 30 pounds heavier than what you put down. And even though you played a 96-year-old man in a college production, do not go in for odd age ranges. Generally you can give yourself a spread of five to ten years without getting into any trouble. Moreover, it helps establish your image if you specify a narrow age range or even simply give your exact age.

As to your credits, your professional experiences are the only really important ones. If you enjoy union affiliation, that fact goes on your résumé right next to your name. If you have acted with a union company, that fact should be at the top of the list. If you have been an extra on a TV pilot, that goes above the Hamlet you did in college. Wherever you have acted with known stars, known directors, known actors, or known theatre companies, be sure that information is clear and dominant. If your experience is limited solely to college or school shows, go ahead and list them blithely, and make sure you act as if they were the most important shows done in the three-state area in which you lived. A sample résumé appears in the Appendix.

Unfortunately, a standard piece of advice is often given young actors preparing a résumé: lie. It is an even bet whether you are better off doing so; you can get caught lying about professional credits, and nobody really cares much about your amateur credits. At times actors have falsely listed roles in productions directed, unknown to them, by the persons to whom they were showing their résumés. The results can be guessed.

A producer once auditioned three women, each one of whom listed the same role in the same production on her résumé. The producer in question merely smiled, knowing the practice was common. However, he also cast another woman in the part. We will not advise you to lie. However, if you understudied Hamlet at Nevada State and ran through it only in the trap room downstairs while the "real" Hamlet was performing on stage, go ahead and list it. The important thing is to list roles that you played and were good at—roles that you could play well again if you were asked.

Things you should *not* include on your résumé are

Your interest or experience in directing

Your membership in Phi Beta Kappa

Your high school or college grades

Your hobbies

Your reasons for wanting a job

Your dedication to acting

Your willingness to do *anything* and *everything*

Your psychological history

Your marital situation

Things you *might* include are

Your special abilities (for example, performance sports, such as high diving, which you do superbly; circus acts, singing and dance experience, nightclub work, and so on).

Your training in acting, singing, dance (listing the names of your instructors if they are well known)

Languages you speak fluently

Dialects you do fluently

Actors vary in what they wish to put on their résumés. The controlling criterion should be what will get a producer or director interested in you. There is no particular "must" format; most agents have their own for their clients, and nobody has come up with a case for or against any one of them. If you want to include a couple of humanizing details (such as your astrological sign), you can do so at the risk of seeming "cutesy"; in general résumés should be clear, simple, and businesslike, and should show your experience at a glance. Don't ever think you can make up for a lack of quality in your credits by substituting quantity. Actors who cram thirty-five amateur roles onto one sheet of paper (or worse, two or three sheets) make it clear that they have been wasting away in the boondocks longer than has been good for them. It is better to show a half-dozen credits that look interesting than five dozen that look repetitious.

Agents and agencies

No character in the theatre or film industry arouses such contradictory attitudes as the agent. To the beginning actor, without contacts and without credits, the agent is the guide to fame and fortune. Actors fall all over themselves trying to get an agent to "represent" them, to put their case over to the moguls in the executive offices, and to do their hatchet work, spade work, telephoning, and interviewing. To the established actor, by contrast, the agent is often a vampire in disguise, sucking the performer's talent and forcing him into commercial ventures devoid of artistic merit, all for 10 percent. A famous actor recently paid his agency a commission of more than $10,000—in pennies, hauled up in an armored truck. Lawsuits and contract-breaking between actors and their agents are unfortunately common in this volatile industry.

Simply speaking, an agent is a person who makes his income by helping you make yours. The agent's job is to get you employment, and for his efforts in doing so, he takes a percentage of your salary. The percentage varies according to the medium. All filmed work performed under a Screen Actors' Guild contract authorizes the agent to take up to 10 percent, and invariably that is what the agent will take. For stage work under Equity auspices, the agent takes only a percentage of the income you make above the Equity minimum. If you are signed to a regional theatre at a union scale (minimum) wage, or even $10 a week more than that, you pay no commission. If you are paid the minimum plus $50, you pay 5 percent for the first 10 weeks. If you are paid the minimum plus $150, you pay 5 percent for the first 6 months, and so forth. As a rule, New York agents do not make very much money representing young actors. That is why you will find that the agent's position there is much less important than in Hollywood. In any case, the agent does not make *any* money unless you do, so that it is entirely to his advantage to get you work and a good price for that work. In theory, one can hardly find fault with such a system.

Still speaking theoretically, an agent works as follows. You agree with an agent (we will discuss how you do this later) that he will represent you, and your agreement is formalized with a contract. Your agent will then take your photographs (which you still provide at your expense) and attach them to new résumés (which he makes up in his agency's format and at his expense). This becomes your photo-résumé, and it lists the agency telephone number and not yours as the contact for all ensuing negotiations. Your agent will then search through whatever casting information is available to him, and will send your photo-résumé to those producers he has reason to feel are looking for someone like you. If your agent is a good one, he will be on the phone all the time with producers looking for specific types of actors or actresses to play specific parts. If you are suitable he will send your photo-résumé for the producer's examination. (These photo-résumés, by the way, are *never* returned, so you had better be prepared to give your agent an inexhaustible supply.) If the producer is interested, he then calls the agent, the agent calls you, and an interview and/or audition is set up at the producer's convenience. The agent will give you whatever information he can get about the part, and if you are a particularly favored client, or he has the time and thinks it would be a good idea, he may personally escort you to the interview, introduce you to the producers, and try in other ways to grease the machinery for you. At that point, however, you are on your own. The interview and audition (or screen test) are all dependent on you. If you come through with flying colors and the producer wants you, he calls the agent back. Here again is a critical step. Your agent and the producer bargain for your salary; surprisingly, perhaps, you find you have little to say about it. If all goes well, your agent will get you the best salary the producer is willing to offer; he then calls you and tells you the terms of your employment. In any case you take the job and when you get paid you give your agent whatever percentage of your *gross* income (the income paid to you before taxes are deducted) that your agency contract specifies. So the actor-agent relationship is a good one when it works. The actor is spending his time perfecting his craft and the agent is hustling up and down Sunset Boulevard or Seventh Avenue looking for the actor's future job. In theory everything is fine, and frequently everything *is* fine.

Here, however, are the bad things that can happen with an agent.

The agent can ignore you. He can take you on with marvelous promises, take a hundred or so photos and résumés, and never talk to you again. When this happens you question why he took you on in the first place. What may have happened is that you have a highly unusual look and the agent is simply going to file your pictures away until he has a call for just that look. Or he took you on as a favor to somebody else who recommended you, or the day after he took you he found someone just like you but "better," or he only wanted to go to bed with you in the first place and you did not give him a chance. There can be any number of reasons why an agent takes you on and then ignores you. If you have not signed a contract with him, you have not lost anything but the photos. Just ignore him and look for somebody else. If you've signed a contract, pester him to death and get him on the stick or get out. Standard Hollywood agency contracts allow you to terminate your obligations if you have not received 15 days work in the past 91 days; in New York, 120 days.

The agent can promote you for the wrong roles. Agents are not simply clearing offices; they are second-guessers. "I admit, we play God," confesses one. And for good reason. They have been in the business, probably a long time, and they think they know how to market you best. (You may be offended at the terms they use: you are part of their "stable" of talent, you are "marketed" like a cabbage, you are a "juvenile female" instead of an actress.) The agent may have as many as fifty actors under contract, and he cannot send them all out for every role. So the agent may send you only for character roles when you think you can play ingenues, and he may or may not be right.

The agent can be too greedy in your behalf. A friend of ours who sings and plays the guitar was offered a terrific contract at a very prestigious New York nightclub, where many celebrities got their starts. He had, however, recently signed with an agent who persuaded him he should get more money. He demanded what she said, the offer was withdrawn, and he has never had the chance again. Other agents go well beyond persuading you to overreach your salary potential; they demand it in your name without even consulting you. Since the agent bargains directly with the producer before you do, he can keep you out of roles you have successfully auditioned for. No matter that you would work for free in order to get that first credit; your agent may negotiate you right out of it by demanding an extra $25. You may see this as just the chance you take—after all, the agent is interested in the same thing you are, right? Not exactly. The agent is interested in your income, which is not always the same as your total artistic and career growth. The best agents are interested in that, too; the greedy ones want their cut and they want it now. Sympathize with them; they have expensive telephone bills. But be alert. Your best interest and theirs are not always exactly the same.

An agent can give you bad advice. In that, he is no more guilty than anybody else you may come across in your pursuit of success, but it hurts more when your agent does it because you feel obligated to take the advice; in fact you probably *are* obligated to take it if you want the agent to help you. Remember that agents are frequently people who would rather have performed themselves, and part of the pleasure they receive from their work is the vicarious thrill of helping, advising, and nurturing others. Agents, after all, do not live a very glamorous life. They spend most of their time contacting studios, bugging receptionists for scraps of information, and being put on HOLD by the secretaries of those producers and casting directors whose names they are dropping. What they lose in personal self-esteem they sometimes make up by treating you the way they are treated by others. In their offices, *they* know all the answers: how you should act, what your pictures should look like, what acting teacher you should study with, how right you are for what role, and how much weight you should lose. Now, in all honesty, we should say that your agent is *probably* right. But the *degree* of probability is not as great as he would have you believe.

We now put the whole thing into perspective with this obvious piece of advice: if you can get an agent, by all means do so. And try and get the very best one for you that you can.

Why is that obvious? The agent is on the inside of the business and you are not. From that point of view, every agent is a good agent; some are more careful, likable, honest, and well-known in the business than others, but all franchised agents have access to important contacts that you do not. In New York, despite the open Equity auditions that the union requires, most casting is done through agencies; in Hollywood all of it is. In Hollywood, only a franchised agent can negotiate a contract with a producer: you cannot. So if you work in New York, you should do what you can to get an agent, or a number of agents, to represent you; and if you work in Hollywood, you absolutely *must* have an agent. Only when you are an established star, and can be confident that producers will call you at *your* telephone number, should you consider going it alone.

Getting an agent

How do you go about getting an agent? The first thing you must do is figure out what kind of agent you want. There are hundreds of agents in both major cities, and they can vary enormously in their worth. The difference between having a career and not having one can quite easily depend on which door you knock on first.

The top agents work in their own offices and handle an absolute minimum of clients. One we know handles only six. You need not worry about him; four of those six make among them more than three million dollars a year and the other two make a few thousand each. Why does he handle the other two at all? Because he expects them to be up with the others in a couple of years. Obviously that is the kind of agent you want. Also obviously, that is not the kind of agent you're going to get. Not yet, anyway.

Other agents work in the huge prestige agencies, of which there are three: Creative Management Associates (CMA), International Famous Agency (IFA, formerly Ashley Famous Agency), and the William Morris Agency.* The big agencies have offices in both New York and Los Angeles; each office may have up to 50 agents who handle the affairs of

*Just prior to publication Creative Management Associates (CMA) and International Famous Agency (IFA) merged to form the International Creative Management (ICM) Agency.

several hundred clients. Not all of these are actors, of course. Some are writers, singers, directors, and musicians, but a large number of them *are* actors, and a lot of those are the people you have heard about since you were twelve. It may do your ego good to be contracted by the same agency that "handles" Jack Nicholson and Cybill Shepherd, but remember that a big agency has big clients, and 10 percent of Jack Nicholson's income means a lot more to them than 10 percent of your income. For this reason the big agencies never (well, almost never) even *look* at an actor until he is already well established and making a sizable income. If you figure that a major agent must book close to half a million dollars worth of business to pay his secretaries, his rent, and his alimony, and have anything left over for his profit, you will realize that only hungry agents are going to take you on when your expectations are still in the subsistence-wage range.

For a young beginning actor, it is almost certainly best to ignore the bigger agencies (which will ignore you in any event) and to hunt out the small, aggressive, hungrier operations that look at untried talent and have the time and inclination to develop a genuine interest in your development. Only then will the actor–agent relationship—a marriage in many ways—prove truly fruitful.

How do you pick a good agent to call on? First of all, the agent *must* be franchised. This means franchised in Hollywood at least by the Screen Actors' Guild, and in New York by the Actor's Equity Association—but preferably with both, and with AFTRA as well. All three union offices will give you lists of their franchised agents, and under no circumstances should you sign with a nonfranchised one. You will know the franchised ones because they'll have a license on the wall. Phony and unlicensed "talent agencies" spring up every year, charge fees (no legitimate agent charges any fee), pressure you into getting highly expensive photographs—usually made by the "talent agent's" brother-in-law for twice the going rate—and go out of business before you realize what has happened. You should also stay away from "artist's managers" or "personal managers" except under rather rare and well-considered circumstances. A personal manager is simply someone who offers to guide your career in return for a percentage of your income. Since he is not an agent, he cannot negotiate a contract, so you will need an agent as well. He is also not likely to have any special qualifications that would give him the ability to assist your career in any way. In a field already dominated by middlemen, the personal manager seems an unnecessary filter between you, your money, your agent, and your art. The only actors who should take on managers, in our opinion, are (1) those in the $100,000-a-year class, who need business guidance, and (2) those in whose future a potential manager has made a substantial cash investment. This should be done as a strict business proposition, and few managers will suggest it. If *you* do, it will certainly test their seriousness about you.

So you have a list of franchised agents. Still, a list is a list. There are currently 167 agencies (not agents—agencies, with one to fifty agents apiece) franchised by Screen Actors' Guild in Hollywood, and 82 Equity-franchised agencies in New York (as well as 54 more New York agencies that are franchised by SAG, AFTRA, or AGVA but not Equity). How do you choose the ones to head for first?

Obviously if you have friends in the industry, you will ask them for suggestions. Beyond that, here is what you can do, and should do in any case. Look at the published listings of actors and their agents that are available in both cities. In Hollywood this is the *Players' Directory*, which is put out three times a year by the Academy of Motion Picture Arts and Sciences. The *Players' Directory* comes out in two huge volumes that look like giant telephone books; they include two pictures of each actor who pays their fee and the name and address of his agent. You can see the *Players' Directory* in the office of any friendly agent, or you can go to the Academy at 9038 Melrose Avenue, Hollywood 90069, and look at the current edition in the reception room. In New York, the equivalent publication is called the *Players Guide*, and it is available at the publisher's office, 165 West 46th Street.

These books are valuable for you to examine merely in order to gauge the competition. You will probably find a depressing number of faces that look pretty good. Look in the pages that list actors of your character type. Find an agency that seems to have a few unknowns in your field. They are good places to start, and if they are over-full in your type, they may recommend you to some agency that is not. By studying these guides, you can get some sort of picture of which agents are handling which kinds of clients, and you will get an idea of where to start.

From these sources you should be able to find the names of ten to fifteen smallish agencies that handle people like yourself and are probably interested in taking on new clients. Perhaps you can rank them in order of desirability, particularly if any of them have been especially recommended by someone you trust. Now you must call on them.

Agents are busy people and they are not going to be eager to see you if you just pop in and announce yourself. In fact, many agents are loath to see *any* inexperienced actor-hopefuls. Unless you do things the right way, you will not get past the receptionist. Here are the time-honored ways of making that first appointment—in order of their effectiveness.

By far the easiest way is through a personal contact. There is the dirty word again, and it is as important as ever. Frankly, most agents will not bother to see *anybody* without a personal reference from someone in the business whom they know. Your best chance of getting an agent, if you can swing it, is to be recommended by a working producer. If a producer is behind you, the agent will feel that you already have a leg up on getting work; besides, by taking you on, the agent may be able to broaden *his* own contacts at the same time. Remember, like you, the agent is always looking to strengthen his contacts. But even if the contact is just another actor who recommends that you see his agent (which, ordinarily, only an actor of the opposite sex is likely to do), the contact is a valuable way to get your foot in the door.

If you lack a personal contact, your next best means of landing an agent is to be *seen* in something. This involves getting a fairly good role in a showcase or workshop production. In New York these are called off-off-Broadway productions; in Los Angeles they are just called workshops. Via agreements with the acting union, workshop productions can be presented for nominal admission fees and for limited runs even though professional actors are used. Getting a good part in one is not by any means automatic, but you can quickly find your way around to their auditions. In New York, the trade papers and *The Village Voice* are good sources of information about the off-off-Broadway market; in Los Angeles the trade papers and the *Los Angeles Free Press* will let you know what is going on. Union offices in both cities are also good sources of casting information for workshop productions.

If you are in a workshop, you will possibly be seen by agents even if you do not do another thing. Part of the agent's job consists of scouting new talent, and these workshop productions are among his chief sources. Productions at the good local colleges (UCLA and USC in Los Angeles; Yale and NYU in New York) are frequently visited by professional agents. But by all means, this is the time for you to contact agents and invite them to come. You will invariably do this first by letter (which you should personally deliver), a letter that includes your photo-résumé and an invitation to see the production at the agent's convenience. You should leave this letter off about two weeks before the production opens and then follow up with a telephone call a few days before opening night.

"Hi," you say in your most unaffected voice, "I'm Tondolaya Schwartzkov, and I left a photo and résumé at your office a couple of weeks ago? . . . Yes . . . and I'd like to see if you would be able to come to see me in *Bloodbath* at the Actors' Experimental Lab any time next week? Friday? I'll leave off the tickets today."

And you do. Hopefully you get several to come on different nights. If they come on the same night, don't worry about it. Let them compete for you. If you are any good, they will be backstage afterward to talk shop with you. See the sample letter on p. 127 of the Appendix for a good example of the right approach to studio or agency personnel.

You need not be in a production for an agent to see you act. A third way of making the agent aware of you is simply to send the agent a letter and a photo-resume and then call and ask for an appointment. Even with no contacts and no chance to see you in performance, an agent could become interested. If you send out a few dozen letters, you should get one or two bites. When you call for an appointment the agent will probably ask you to perform a scene in his office, and if he likes it, and you, a working relationship may be forthcoming.

Interviewing an agent

Once you have finally contacted an agent, he will ask you to his office for an interview, at which he will determine whether or not to take you on. Since you will be interviewing for most of the roles you will get, you must treat the interview with the agent just as seriously as an interview with a producer or director. The agent will be trying to see if you interview as well as you act, and it is important that you impress upon him that you do.

If you are invited to "come in and talk," set up an appointment and keep it exactly. Come on time, and come in looking your best. If you look your best in jeans and a Mickey Mouse T shirt, wear them, but be clean, neat, and striking. "Look like an actor and act like an actor," cautions one agent. Be at ease and be yourself. Agents are not always very good at interviewing people; they are apt to be unsure of what to ask and generally nervous. Help the agent interview you. Tell him about your career, your desires, your commitment, your training, what you feel you can do, and what sacrifices you are prepared to make. Answer his questions truthfully. An agent is like a lawyer: you have to trust him completely. If there is any lying to be done about your career, you will want him to do it, not you. Impress on the agent that you want to become a working professional actor, and that you have a realistic outlook about your future. Do not presume to know more than he does about show business, even if you think you do. Terminate the interview when you think you have said and asked everything on your mind. Some people do not know when to quit talking, and some agents do not know how to get people out of their offices. Offer to leave when you sense the interview is over, and go home or see a movie.

The agent will rarely offer you a contract on the spot. He may want to think you over, to consult with colleagues, and to check his files for available jobs in your category. If he wants you, he will let you know, either by grabbing you before you leave the office or by calling you later. Your task is simply to keep trying until someone grabs you.

Occasionally the agent will ask you to do a scene in his office, particularly if he has never seen you act. In this case, be prepared to do so. You will be doing so often in your career, and this is a good time to get started. See the section on prepared scenes, pp. 89–94, those principles apply here.

Eventually an agent will decide to take you on as a client. In Hollywood you will sign an exclusive contract for the agent to represent you in all dramatic camera media. This is a regulation of the Screen Actors' Guild; only a franchised agent can negotiate a contract, and an actor may be represented by only one franchised agent. You can, if you so desire, have another agent for commercials, and another for live theatre, but frequently in Hollywood you will simply have one agent who will handle you in all media. In New York the practice is somewhat different. There agents may take you on without signing you to exclusive contracts. An actor in New York may have working agreements (written or otherwise) with any number of agents at the same time. In New York, where an actor can get along fairly well without an agent at all, the agent's position is more that of a booking agent; he has a roster of jobs that he tries to apportion among a roster of clients before another agent gets to them. New York agents hustle a lot, as a result, but it is also easy to get lost in the shuffle of their rosters. It is desirable, therefore, to establish a solid, trusting relationship with a New York agent, one who is deeply committed to you and your success.

If you sign with an agent, or have an agent working for you, you have entered into a partnership that it is hoped will prove beneficial to both of you. At this point you have by no means "made it"; you are still just beginning. If your agent is a good one, he will take a profound interest in your career. He will advise you about photographs, he will make up your new résumé, and he will try to introduce you to the right people at the right time. He will get your pictures into the *Players' Directory* or *Players' Guide* (though you pay the fee). He will manage your career. It is vital that you establish a trusting relationship. This takes patience on your part. Frequently an actor signs with an agent, and then, three months later, having had no significant results, he starts shopping for another. The business does not work that way. Your agent will need time to get to know you and your work; he will try to establish your image together with his own in the memory of the producers with whom he comes in contact. One agent estimates that it takes about a year for the agent to really establish his client in the overall market picture, and another two years to get offers coming in with any regularity—and that is if things go well. The third year, he says, is usually when the payoff comes, if it does. The actor who impatiently switches agents over and over again merely starts anew each time and never has the chance to establish an image in the industry.

Each agent, however, has his own point of view, and an agent whose plan to market you is a bad one is ultimately of little use to you. You want an agent who, whatever his standing, is enthusiastic about you and sees you pretty much the way you want to be seen. If you want to play classical tragedy and he wants to sell you for *Kung Fu*, you had better get things straight before you sign. No agent will be offended if you simply ask: "How do you see me?" Let him tell you; you may be astonished at what he sees. Give him the benefit of the doubt, if there is one. You might be a lot better in *Kung Fu* than in *King Lear*. On the other hand, you may not want to spend the rest of your life with *Kung Fu* and its ilk, so you have some decisions to make.

If you are lucky enough to find an agent who sees you the way you wish to be seen, take him and do what he says. Accept his judgment on your photographs, what you should wear, how you should do your hair, how much weight you should lose, and so forth. Talk things over, but be prepared to trust him. Nobody's advice is *perfect*, but your agent is your partner, and the two of you had better be working together and not at odds with each other.

Unfortunately, when you get your first agent, there is a terrible temptation to settle back and wait for the jobs to come pouring in. Nothing could be worse. You are still going to have to make your rounds, get yourself known, get involved, and hustle up contacts. You're also going to have to hustle your own agent! As William Bayer explains, *"Hustle your hustler.* You're going to have to sell and pressure and hustle just as much with an agent as without one; you're going to have to continue to excite your agent, because the moment he gets bored, there's nothing in it for either of you."* Look into the human nature of this situation: if the agent mentions your name to a hundred casting directors, and three or four go "Hmmm . . . yeah, I remember him from . . ." then your agent feels encouraged about your chances (and his 10 percent). If he gets a hundred blank stares, he may start doubting the wisdom of having taken you on. Help him along. Meet people. That means the time-honored "rounds."

Rounds

What does the actor do all day when he is not working? He goes on his rounds. This is as time-honored as the opening night party at Sardi's.

* *Breaking Through, Selling Out, Dropping Dead,* p. 22.

With a good pair of shoes, or a good clutch in the Volkswagen, the actor goes to see everybody and anybody who can get him a job in the theatre.

Rounds in New York are much more part of an actor's daily routine than they are in Hollywood, and an actor there can go out on rounds without an agent or a union card to pave the way. The goal of making rounds is to see as many producers and agents as possible and make them aware of your presence and your availability. You should first check the regular casting notices posted on the Equity office bulletin board (1500 Broadway) and in the casting pages of *Variety*, *Backstage*, and *Show Business*, and then visit the producers' offices with copies of your photo-résumé to leave off. You can follow up these visits with a call or repeat visit to see if any action has been taken yet. You will rarely get further than the receptionist's office, but do not despair. Making rounds is an ego-busting trip anyway, and you must not let it get to you. The receptionist generally will transmit whatever material you give her, and if there is a chance for you, you will hear about it.

After going to the producers you know are casting, you head for those about whom you know nothing. You can simply look up the names of active producers and agents in the yellow pages of the Manhattan Telephone Directory and follow them up. Or better, you can take a walk over to the Drama Book Shop (150 West 52nd Street) and purchase a current *Geographic Casting Guide* ($1.75). This guide, revised every six months or so, lists all the New York agents, producers, and casting directors (advertising and television) by street address, so that you can hit the 37 offices on 57th street without retracing a step. This little book is worth a mint in saving you time and blistered toes. The Drama Book Shop is also a worthwhile regular stop on your daily rounds; the bulletin board sporadically lists casting opportunities, and the shop, which sells virtually every theatre publication available in English, offers a superb collection of fact sheets, pamphlets, and books that are helpful to theatre people like yourself.

In Hollywood, your rounds are mainly restricted to producers of commercials; the producers of television and film shows are accessible only by an appointment arranged by your agent. (Many New York producers are available solely in that fashion too.) But the commercial producers are many, and many can be visited without an appointment. Get a list from your agent or from *Simon's Directory of Theatrical Materials, Services and Information* and map yourself out an itinerary. It is desirable to call commercial agencies first and ask for an appointment; you can still manage to see several in a day's time if you avoid rush hours and long crosstown trips. One discouraging note, maybe: a Screen Actors' Guild union card (see Unions, p. 100) is almost essential for commercial work, unless you have some highly specialized ability or characteristic that they need. With your SAG card, however, and a good photo-résumé, you might get somewhere in the commercial field, which can not only make you a lot of money (residual payments frequently go into the thousands and tens of thousands for long running commercials) but also will allow you to be seen by thousands of producers when they watch Johnny Carson after work. Not a few actors have gotten their first real break after being seen in a bright, novel "commersh."

Hollywood is a more guarded, more private place than New York, with rigid screening institutionalized by agents and studios, but there's no reason you shouldn't try to break through those walls if you can do it gracefully. A young Hollywood aspirant who writes that "Contacts are everything," explains the success of one of his friends:

[X is] an actor who works a lot and has taught me a great deal. He works a lot because he *never* stops plugging. He makes job hunting a full-time occupation. He has excellent agents, but he gets himself one-half of his jobs! Everyday he goes to one studio to drop by to just say 'hi' to the casting people—so he will be fresh in their minds. He reads the trades every day to see what new projects are beginning and who is involved. He then immediately goes to see them, no matter how big they are (both Robert Wise and Mike Nichols have thrown him out of their offices!). He's got a lot of *chutzpah*—a true necessity. All these things he's taught me I now do too. I've become very daring, and now march right through (or drive right through) the studio gates. I've learned that you can go *anywhere* if you look like you belong, so I simply wave at the studio guard as I enter the studio and he waves back.

Thus rounds become the day-to-day lifestyle of the actor in New York or Hollywood.

Getting known: advertisements for yourself

Rounds are a form of self-advertisement. So is getting your picture into *Player's Guide*. So is showcasing yourself in an off-off-Broadway production (or Hollywood workshop) and inviting agents, casting directors, and other professionals to see your work. Show business and politics are the media of the one-man advertisements; if you look through the pages of *Variety*, you may get the impression that an election is in progress, and in some ways you will be right. For actors huckster themselves blithely and boldly, and sometimes with direct results.

The most discreet advertising is done by stars, who pay high fees to the public relations experts managing their affairs. This may consist of taking space in *Variety* to "congratulate" the magazine on its anniversary (and make clear the star is still alive, kicking, and available) or seizing a charity that will keep the star's name before the public, and raise the standard of her or his reputation. Neither of these possibilities of self-advertisement is open to you. (The first would not only be presumptuous, it would probably not even be looked at twice—as for the second, your charitable contribution will be accepted with thanks, but not publicity.) For the young actor a direct advertisement tied to a successful appearance in a showcase is sometimes worthwhile. Elaine Partnow, a Los Angeles actress, capitalized on her 1973 performance in an LA workshop production by putting together some of her reviews, which were in the "brilliant" category, and putting them into a quarter-page ad in (Daily) *Variety*. Then she made up 800 reproductions of the ad and sent them to every producer and director in television, and every Equity theatre in the country. The total cost for this advertisement and mailing was about $175. The result "Two phone calls." At a hundred bucks a call, that's an expensive way to get known. But it might work and it's tried all the time. After all, it only takes *one* phone call if it's the right one. Some self-advertising hopefuls go to extraordinary lengths. An Alma Kessler, not too long ago, paid $10,000 to put her face (six times lifesize) on billboards over Sunset Boulevard, with the leading line "Who is Alma Kessler and what's her game?" "Why?" she was asked. "I love show business. I've always wanted to be a performer. I'm 50, and I'm free, it's now or never. I've got to be a star. So it costs money? So what's money?" Taking out an advertisement for oneself can be an expensive and sometimes humiliating experience. But one must get known and sometimes it's "now or never."

Interviews

Interviews are as much a make-or-break step on the road to getting a role as any other single act. The interview takes place when the producer has called *you* (as contrasted to your rounds, where you are calling on him). Thus, with an interview, you at least know you are in contention for something, even though hundreds of others may share your status. In Hollywood, particularly, the majority of roles are cast solely on the basis of interviews; in fact, working professional film actors make it a point of personal privilege never to audition; they simply meet the producer, who either is already familiar with their work or can call up film on the actors from the vaults. But if you have not worked, or you are in New York, the interview is merely a milepost on the road to an audition. And you must pass the milepost with élan.

Interviews are a great stumbling block for many actors. "I don't interview well" is a common complaint, and actors who have been trained to play characters with strength, compassion, and subtlety fall completely to pieces when they are asked to play themselves. For that is what you do in an interview: you play yourself. You must not pretend for a moment that an interview is simply a casual, obligatory preface to an audition. The interview is a stage on which million-dollar decision are made, and despite the general and desirable state of informality, you are being examined very closely—and you must perform.

The interview is calculated to let the producer know just what kind of person you are. As we discussed earlier, film and television directors rely heavily on your personality rather than your acting ability. "Casting people are afraid of people who *act*," is an often-voiced Hollywood complaint, and doubtless this is in many cases true. Because of the extremely limited rehearsal time for most television shows (and many films and plays, for that matter), producers are always partial to the actor whose own personality closely matches the characterization they want. Remember too, they have literally thousands of people to choose from; why should they take someone 6'3" when they want, and can easily get, someone who's 6'2"? Casting decisions are rarely that specific as to height, but if you translate that into subjective qualities, you begin to see how little compromise they have to make.

How do you perform in an interview? You play yourself, to be sure, but you are entitled to select which aspects of yourself you want to display. Be yourself, but be your *best* self. You are an actor: look like it and act like it. You are a professional: let them know it. Arrive on time, prepared with your photo-résumé and a book of pictures of yourself. Relax and let your salable qualities shine. Ask questions. Be vivacious, not retiring. Be friendly but not self-effacing. Be funny, if you feel like it, but not at your own (or their) expense. In short, sell yourself without blasting them out of the room.

What will you face? Usually one producer—maybe two or three; maybe a casting director or two; and maybe a secretary or another actor who happens to be in the room with you. You will be introduced to everyone; try to remember their names (and, when you leave the office, write them down for future reference). Your first look when you walk in the door tells them 75 percent of what they wanted to know already. Make it a good look. Be confident, be attractive, and show those things which you consider your personal assets. Then sit down and get them to talk to you.

Without fail you will be asked, "Well, tell me about yourself." There it is: the one big identity question that has shrivelled some actors into their own neuroses so far that they can only stammer their name, rank, and social security number. Be prepared for it. There are no rules for interviews, no forms to fill out. If you begin by telling them all your problems, the interview is over before it begins. "Well, I suppose you want to know about my credits. I don't have any." Only a psychologist can explain why so many actors destroy themselves daily by such remarks. Tell them about yourself honestly but positively: "I want to become a working professional actor . . . I played *Coriolanus* at Ashland . . . I'm a short story writer with *Argosy* magazine." Tell them things you would like them to know and avoid things you would rather they did not know. Nobody has asked you to present both sides of the case, and believe us, they have every reason in the world *not* to cast you, so don't make that decision any easier for them.

Producers see a great many people when they are casting, so it certainly does not hurt to be memorable. If you can look memorable, or say something memorable, or do something memorable, it helps. Mere politeness (which, after all, you must practice) is not enough to stimulate anybody's interest; everybody is polite. While it is hardly recommended, a downright hostile attitude at the end of a wearying day has sometimes aroused a little excitement in a casting director, although it rarely has produced an actual offer. Find an exciting way to be different.

Interviewing takes some practice. No amount of advice is helpful after the first few interviews, because everyone must find his own style of "being himself" and being himself memorably. You should go to every interview you possibly can, because with each you will acquire not only valuable know-how, but a confidence that is necessary and that you can never fake. It takes most people ten or fifteen interviews before they finally start to "come out," since the tendency of most sensitive people (and most actors are sensitive people) is to sit docilely in an overstuffed chair and answer the questions they are asked as simply as possible. If you breathe a sigh of relief when an interview is over, you probably have not done a very good job. Conversely, if you feel you have met some interesting people, then they probably feel the same way about you, and you probably have done well.

Here's a stream-of-consciousness report on the subject from a young actor currently making headway in his career:

Initial office report, the complexity of the office—well it's difficult to get on to it but you MUST get right on to it, right away. It's a fine line, a very fine line. You have to be up, funny, likable, charming, and impressive, and yet a little bit vulnerable, and hopefully a tiny bit naive, but you can't think about *any* of that, you just have to be your own natural self, and you're being eyeballed every second—they just want to hear you talk, and that's why so many lead-off questions are "Hi, Bruce, tell me about yourself!" What could be worse? You don't know where to start. "Well, I'm a new actor, new in town, and I hope for the best . . ." No one wants to hear that, but what they want to hear is a relaxed, calm, involved person; an "on" person. But you can't be too on, too up—well, this all has to be learned. Some love it, some hate it. I love it because I'm into people and I love people and that's where you meet them—all sorts of new people—in the office.

Here's another, from a similarly successful young actor two years into a professional career:

> Perhaps the most important thing I have learned in working professionally is that "to succeed" the prime ingredient is confidence. That is not overconfidence or bravura or telling everyone what a success you're going to be. The confidence I'm talking about is an inner trust, acceptance, and knowledge of yourself. Casting agents, directors, producers, and everyone else in the business generally aren't terribly concerned about your being the next Laurence Olivier. What they are concerned with is: are you real, responsible, confident of what you can do and of your limitations, relaxed, dependable, and pleasant to work with and talk to, and of course whether you have the look and quality they happen to be looking for. Time and time again friends of mine have told me how they've gotten a job when they least expected it. Usually that's because they had gone to an interview or an audition not really expecting to get the part (which is not to say they were unprepared!) and were so relaxed that their natural qualities and abilities came out to their best advantage. Their attitude was *professional*, and most importantly, professional in a natural, relaxed way.

So go in there and have a good time and be yourself. And get to know the secretaries and receptionists. You need all the friends you can find.

Auditions

Auditions are the means by which the stage actor and the beginning film actor show the producers what they can do. If you are at the beginning of your career, it is absolutely essential that you learn to audition and to audition well. Again, actors have all sorts of hangups about auditions, and many feel they audition poorly but act magnificently. If that is your hangup, you will have to get over it. Producers with thousands of actors to choose from do not need to bother having faith in you. They will choose someone who they *know* can do the role, and they know it on the basis of his superior audition.

There are two types and two locations for auditions. The types are the prepared scene and the cold reading. The locations are the producer's office and the stage. You must be prepared for all four combinations.

Prepared scenes are the actor's opportunity to show himself at his very best. Every aspiring actor should have many prepared scenes always at the ready. Often you will have a chance to audition when you least expect it, and you should always have a few pieces up your sleeve. For stage work your audition pieces should be monologues. The TCG auditions specify two contrasting pieces totalling in combination no more than four minutes in length; one in verse and one in prose, one pre-nineteenth century and one contemporary or relatively contemporary. This general format is standard for most LORT auditions, as well as URTA auditions and many others. While it is not required that either piece be a comedy, it is usually quite helpful if one is—casting directors who may hear dozens of monologues in a three-hour casting session are ordinarily quite grateful for something that is genuinely funny, witty, or charming among all the Medeas and Hamlets. For film and television auditions you should prepare scenes with a partner rather than monologues, and with a partner who will generally be available for fast-breaking opportunities that may arrive in the future. Choose your scenes and rehearse them carefully. In preparing for prepared auditions, you should keep the following in mind:

Brevity is essential. While four minutes is the TCG maximum, that does not make 3:59 the minimum. Film and TV scenes can usually peak in three to four minutes. Your scene must be long enough to build, to produce an impact—but then it must end. Though few actors are aware of it, the producer generally gets all the information he wants in the first few seconds of your audition; the rest of the time he is quite possibly thinking of something (or someone) else.

The prepared scene should show you in a role in which you could be cast *today*. Particularly if you are auditioning for a film or television role, do something very close to your age and personality, and something in a style as close as possible to the style of the part for which you are auditioning. If you are auditioning at Screen Gems, it is silly to do a scene from *Othello*. Even if you played old ladies in college, you will not do them on Broadway, so don't give them your Aunt Eller until you are in your fifties.

Choose audition material that is self-explanatory. In no case should you explain, before your audition, the plot of the scene or the characterization you are trying to convey. At most you should say the name of the scene and proceed. Choose scenes that do not require specific pieces of furniture, properties, or extensive movement, scenes which you could present in a variety of locations and without bringing a suitcase full of production aids.

Choose audition material that is not shopworn. Every year there are a few "in" audition pieces that generally mean instant death for the poor actor doing them before a group that has seen them 50 times. It is fun and frequently rewarding to find scenes in contemporary novels and extract them for audition material; chances are the dialogue is realistic and the auditioners will be interested in seeing something new. Remember, they are judging you, not the material, and it does not have to be a masterpiece for them to like you doing it.

Preparedness is, of course, important. How much should you prepare? There is no easy answer to that question: you can be overrehearsed, but you can never be overprepared. Preparation is what gives you confidence and calm—it takes your mind off yourself and lets you concentrate on the business at hand. A relaxed preparedness is perhaps the most professional attitude you can bring to an audition. When George C. Scott first decided he wanted to become an actor, he decided to read for the leading part in a campus production. Getting a copy of the script, he memorized the entire part, word for word, before the audition. "They were flabbergasted, nobody had ever bothered to learn the part for an audition. I got the role." This should be a model. All too frequently actors refuse to prepare on the grounds that it will rob them of spontaneity or casualness, but we think it takes little objective contemplation to realize that spontaneity and casualness are the result of careful, not shoddy preparation. And that sort of preparation—even if you fail to get the role—is never wasted.

Prepare your scenes under the various circumstances in which you may have to perform them. Rehearse on large stages and in small, office-like rooms. Rehearse with a "director" watching you, or try out your audition piece as often as you can in an acting class, at a party, in your home, or wherever you can get an audience of one or more to see you. Get used to performing amidst general inattention and extraneous noise. Rehearse and prepare your introduction to your scene, your transition between one monologue and the next, and even the "thank you" with which you conclude your audition. Obvious unpreparedness is instant death in a prepared-scene audition, for if you have not taken the time and energy to work on your audition, how can you demonstrate your willingness to expend time and energy on your part?

Keep your scenes loose, and not dependent on any single planned "effect." Let the environment of your performance, whether it be office or stage, affect what you and your partner do. Preparation does not necessarily mean rehearsing and fixing every movement and gesture of a scene; some actors prefer to prepare the lines of a scene only, and leave the physical and emotional actions free and unrehearsed. This is particularly useful for film and television auditions, and in fact more closely duplicates the way these scenes would be shot professionally than stage rehearsing would. Remember, in an audition the producer is not looking for a completed performance, but for your ability to act convincingly (and, when you have a partner, to *re*act convincingly, as well).

Choose your acting partner carefully. You must trust him completely. He should be willing to give you focus if it is your audition. You might respond by working up some scenes in which he has focus for his auditions. But no matter whose scene it is, you look better if he is good than if he is bad, so do not grab a bad partner in the hope that he will make you look good.

If you are permitted, or required, to do two scenes, choose two that differ in tone and style rather than in age. Generally you are asked to do contrasting scenes, such as comedy and drama, or (particularly with stage work) classical and modern. Do not think of these categories as absolute, and do not worry too much about whether *Tartuffe* is funny or serious or whether *St. Joan* is modern or classical. The point is to get two differing scenes that show you off to your best advantage. If you are confused about what kinds of scenes they want, ask.

Above all, choose material that shows you at your best. Ultimately, that is your overriding concern. You do not want your audition scenes to be merely good; you want them to be terrific. Choose material at which you excel, even if it means not doing exactly what they have asked or we have suggested. The audition fails if you do not come off looking better than anybody they have seen that day, and a merely competent job with material you do not like is as bad as nothing at all. Have your agent preview your audition pieces and comment. If you are doing a full stage audition, such as the Chicago auditions, by all means get a director to help you and work on your audition until you are satisfied that it shows off your best qualities.

In giving your audition, take the stage. Take and claim your space. You may know from experience that you're likely to be interrupted six bars into your song, or fifteen seconds into your monologue, but put that out of your mind. For those fifteen seconds or five minutes, dominate the stage you are on and make it your own; for if you do not trust yourself, why should they?

Direct your audition at the auditioners, not at your fellow actors who might be in the same room. This particularly applies to group auditions like those sponsored by TCG at Chicago. At the Chicago auditions the center of the house is filled with regional theatre producers and directors, and the auditioning actors are seated in a pocket of seats near the corner of the stage. Many of those auditioning direct their focus toward the auditioning actors rather than the directors. This is easy to understand, for while the other actors might be one's competition, they are also of one's social and professional level; they "feel better"; they are a "safe" audience. Unfortunately this falling back onto one's peers shows through as timidity, and it tends to create a weak audition. Far more successful are the actors who seize the stage and give every impression that they have turned their backs forever on the "youngsters" behind them. This may sound cruel, in a way, but it is simply part of the growing up and growing out that an actor must finally do.

Dress for the audition. It is not necessary, and in fact it is sometimes downright hurtful, to costume yourself fully for the part you're reading for, at least during your first audition. But it is vitally important to *look* the part. The reason you shouldn't fully costume yourself (emphasis here is on the "fully") is twofold; it will probably make you uncomfortable, and it may also make you look a bit desperate. But if you have wardrobe items that are generally wearable on the street as well as perfect for the part, then by all means wear those clothes. In other words, look the part without looking like you're *trying* to look the part.

When you are auditioning for TCG, or for regional theatres that are looking at you as a potential company actor rather than for any particular role, you should dress like a professional actor. That does *not* mean to dress like a college actor. As a rule, college actors are poorer and dress in a more slovenly way than professional actors. Let's face it; professional directors make good incomes, have American Express cards, stay in good hotels, eat in expensive restaurants, and associate mainly with *employed* actors who also dress and live fairly well. Regardless of what we might think of the artistic temperament, the lifestyle of most regional theatre directors (and for that matter New York and Hollywood directors) is fairly conservative, and fairly middle class. Ripped jeans, bare feet, and stained T shirts just don't have the same effect on the TCG stage as they do in the State University Experimental Theatre. You, of course, have every right to be yourself, and dress as you choose, and nobody will *think* he is judging you on the basis of your clothing (much less say so), but to "dress down" (even if you simply cannot afford to dress "up") is to create a certain alienation that your audition may not overcome. The image of disaffected youth is not one that you want to project in a general audition. Even if you seek to become the long awaited "next James Dean," you had better learn to be comfortable in "grownup" attire. Actors and actresses are not looked down upon in the least for auditioning in dresses, sportcoats, handsome sweaters, shined shoes, and sharp outfits. These are not at all *necessary*, but they will lead you to a quicker and higher degree of rapport with people who, after all, dress more or less the same way.

One final word on clothes: You must be comfortable in them. If you are only comfortable in tattered campus gear, then that's what you're going to have to wear until and unless you get accustomed to something better. You can't worry about the way you look, or *they'll* start to worry about the way you look. And, of course, that's murder.

Auditions and interviews are both competitions, and you must treat them as such. You are being examined for your usefulness in an industry that wants to make money by your efforts. There are many competitors for every job; they are, in effect, put on a treadmill and passed in front of the casting directors and producers. It is your task to stop the treadmill and make the auditioners take notice of your individual value to their enterprise. Whatever you can do (within the bounds of your own personality and ethics) to accomplish that, you ought to do.

Prepared scenes versus cold readings

Prepared scenes are generally requested when the actor has not been seen. TCG, regional repertory companies, and most New York theatre producers will see prepared scenes at regular intervals, ordinarily at the request of an actor or his agent. Agents frequently ask to see prepared scenes from actors they are interested in representing. Most Hollywood casting offices set aside one or two days a month to see prepared audition scenes from new talent referred to them by agents. Except in the case of those regional repertory auditions, where actors are hired for an entire season at a time, prepared scene auditions rarely lead directly to employment. Most often they serve simply to introduce the actor to producers who might some day want to use him. Most audition scenes are viewed without respect to specific casting availabilities.

Cold readings are the next step toward a job. In a cold reading you are called in, given a copy of a script, and asked to read it and act it for the producers. In a cold reading, you are going for a specific part, and at least you know that a part exists. If you are right for it, you may get it. You read, either alone or with the stage manager, the producer, or another actor auditioning for another role, and you stop when you are told. Your reading may be on a stage or in an office. Your object, quite obviously, is to be overwhelmingly good.

A cold reading need not be entirely cold, and if the idea of cold readings frightens you (and it should), there is plenty you can do about it. Ordinarily you can read the script beforehand—perhaps in the office waiting room. Sometimes you can get the script the day before. Generally they will at least offer you the chance to skim the text, and naturally you should take it. If not, you can always ask a couple of questions. Frequently actors feel they should not ask the director what he wants. Directors, however, are paid to answer actors' questions. Certainly you should make sure of the character's basic intentions, age, and characteristics if they are not evident in what you see. Try to put that all into one question, and then let the director talk as long as he wishes.

Do not worry if you cannot pronounce certain words or if you muff lines. Nobody expects a finished performance at a cold reading, and no good directors care at this point for perfection of detail. What they are looking for is that germ of characterization they find essential to the part. If you have it, and they are confident you can get the rest in the time available, you will be in the running. If, however, you get flustered merely because you cannot pronounce the character's name, your lack of confidence may ruin your performance.

It is best to avoid heavy characterization in a cold reading, unless you are *certain* that is what is required. If you are not, be as natural as possible; read the character as if he were you, or you were he, and let the director see your basic personal quality in your acting. If the role requires a dialect and you can do it, do it; if you can't, don't. In general do not try anything that may make you look bad unless they ask you to do so.

Most cold readings are terminated by the director when he has found out what he wants to know. Sometimes, however, he seems uncertain. He doesn't ask you to leave, but you can tell that he is not entirely satisfied, either: He is making up his mind. This is a good time to ask him, for example, "Do you think in this scene Martha would be a little more compassionate?" You might get a little direction and a chance to do it again in a manner closer to the director's idea of the part. Remember, the director cannot read your mind, and he probably assumes that if you did not read the role with more compassion, it was because you could not. Both directors and actors have an odd way of assuming that their interpretations are universally understood. Always look for any information you can get on what the director or producer wants, and use it. If he coaches you, listen. Unless you are quite certain of your indispensability, this is not the time to debate his points.

If you sing, you may be invited to audition for musical plays or films. You should be prepared to sing a song or two for the producers, and if you can get the music to one of the songs in the production being done, do so. You should bring your own music to a musical audition, properly marked for the transpositions and tempos that you wish to use. You may wish to hire your own accompanist to rehearse with you and accompany you. This is standard practice in all professional auditions, since poor accompaniment (even from a good musician who simply has not rehearsed with you) can ruin your presentation.

Sometimes in an audition or an interview you will be asked to take off your clothes. Contemporary films frequently involve nudity, and so, increasingly, does contemporary theatre. There are strict union regulations regarding this, and you should be aware of them. It is entirely proper for a director to get some idea of what your body looks like, and he might ask you to show him without having you undress. Under no circumstances, however, may he ask you to undress without having informed you when the appointment was made that the part involves nudity and that you will be asked to disrobe during audition. This at least gives you time to check out the producer and make sure you know what you are getting into. Remember that your agent and the union (even if you are not a member) will protect you from unscrupulous voyeurs who happen to be producing films and plays. On the other hand, if you plan to do nude films or plays, you had better plan on doing nude auditions as well.

You will have to adopt a pretty stable audition attitude. Like everything else in the life of a beginning professional actor, auditions can lead to paranoia. Even if everybody from the producer on down is extremely polite, you are nevertheless unceremoniously directed to perform when they ask you and to leave when they tell you. Frequently you are ushered onto a stage and see nothing in front of you but bright lights and a few shadowy forms at the back, and you hear nothing but "Name!" "Well, let's see it!" and, in the middle of your prepared monologue, "Thank you very much. Next please!" It is discouraging to the strong and ruinous to the weak, and you had better be prepared for it. A professional attitude is your point of strength. Remember always that you have to stop the treadmill. Only if you are solidly confident can you be strong enough to do that.

The screen test

Screen tests are used in Hollywood to see how you look on camera. The screen test may be a very simple affair whereby you turn your face from left to right in front of a camera and speak some lines or improvise a conversation. Or it can be as involved as a complete scene that you rehearse with a studio director and perform with sets and costumes. For major roles in films and television series, the screen test is usually the last stage of the audition, and the finalists for a certain role may screen-test opposite each other. Only newcomers are screen-tested, however, since veteran actors can be seen by studio executives in actual film or taped performances available to them on call.

Screen tests are not universally used any more, and many producers have no time for them at all. Paul Monash cast Michael Sacks, a 22-year-old actor with no professional acting experience whatever, as the lead in *Slaughterhouse Five* without a test, declaring he did not believe in them. Nevertheless, be prepared to do a screen test, since you might well be asked for one. Naturally the more experience you have had before a camera, the better, so seize every opportunity to perform and see yourself in student films and even home movies.

The job offer

If you have played all your cards right, if you are as good as you think you are, and if your contacts, interviews, auditions, and readings have gone well, you may be offered a part. You now have to decide whether you will take it or not. For most actors, this is the easiest decision of their lives.

There are some jobs, however, that you might want to think twice about taking, even if they are the first thing that comes your way.

The job could be a non-union job. Many theatres and independent film companies skirt union regulations and jurisdiction. Even though they may pay you a union scale wage, they do not operate according to certain procedures that the union requires of all producers. Check with the union. If the producer is operating in frank violation of union regulations, you may find yourself blackballed from future employment. This is rare, but investigate. If it happens to you, you may never live it down.

The job could be quasi-union. That is, it could be a workshop or experimental production (student films come under this category) that operates under a special dispensation from the union. In this case you are liable not to be paid, or to be given "deferred payment," which means you will not get the money until the project is successfully marketed. If the project is non-union but operated in accordance with the union, you have nothing to fear from participating, but you might not get more out of it than the work itself.

The job could be union but distant. For example, you could be hired for two months in June to work bit parts at an Equity dinner theatre in

Williamsburg, Virginia. So while you are carrying spears and inviting the guests to dinner in Virginia (for a salary that doesn't permit you to keep your New York digs) you're missing important Broadway and off-Broadway auditions in the city.

The job could be a nudie film or play. These come in two categories. The independent non-union X-rated films (and stage equivalents) are utterly useless to you except as a source of income, and the income is pretty low. The days are over when an actress had her career ruined because she posed in the nude, but we have not reached the point when her career would be particularly helped by being featured in one of the fellatio flicks. Even the major studio pornographic films offer little besides more money and a chance to roll around with some attractive strangers in the nude.

Then there are "serious" nude films, or rather, serious films that have nude sequences. Every young actor today, particularly in films, should expect to be asked, sometime early in his career, to do a nude scene. The answer that most will give—that they will do it as long as it is tastefully done—is not really to the point, since the producer will invariably tell you that it will be tastefully done, and until the final cut you have no idea exactly what that means; and, possibly, neither does he. At any rate, do not for a moment think that "if they want me badly enough, they'll get a double for the nude scenes." They will not want you that badly.

Doing nude scenes in films may be even harder than you think. If it were a matter of simply flipping off a robe, shooting a quick scene, and then dressing again, that would be one thing. More often, even for a simple ten-second shot, many hours of takes and retakes will be required. You might find yourself standing, sitting, and lying around in the nude amidst fifty technicians, actors, and producers (all fully dressed) while they take, focus, retake, and refocus your ten-second nude scene. Strong, uninhibited actresses have been reduced to quivering tears by this dehumanizing process, which, after all, is exactly the device the Nazis used to humiliate and interrogate political prisoners.

The role may be otherwise offensive. It may be pornographic, or simply too small, or the style of the material may be too clichéd and ridiculous for your taste and talent. You may be asked to work with actors or directors you do not respect, or in a television show you loathe. You may be asked to do a commercial for a product you find personally disgusting, or to do a dialect you find ethnically or racially degrading.

There are, then, a number of possible reasons why you might not choose to accept every job that comes your way, and why you might want to wait until the "right one" comes along. For every acceptance ties you up and holds you back from possibilities not yet known. But this is mainly cavil. Lucille Ball once said that the way she got to the top of her profession was by taking absolutely every job she could get. Tony Curtis was quoted in *Variety*, as saying, "I think anybody in this business should take any job he can get today." Jason Robards says, "The only advice I have for young people is, no matter how you do it, do it in front of people who pay."* There is more than just an immediate reason for this. It's that one job begets another: power begets power. A fine actor of our acquaintance worked steadily for ten years, at which time he looked back and realized that every single job he had (except the first) evolved out of a previous one. A beginning actor, therefore, should refuse a union job only for extraordinarily compelling reasons.

Unions

If you accept a union job, you will now join the appropriate union. The three dramatic unions, which have been mentioned frequently herein, are the Screen Actors' Guild (SAG), which handles all filmed acting (including filmed television shows and filmed commercials); Actors' Equity Association, which handles all live theatre performing, and the American Federation of Television and Radio Artists (AFTRA), which handles all live and videotaped television programming and commercials, as well as radio broadcasting. These unions are joined together with a few others in a loose association referred to as the Associated Actors and Artists of America (the Four A's), which also includes the American Guild of Variety Artists (AGVA), the American Guild of Musical Artists (AGMA), and the Screen Extras' Guild (SEG). The unions seem a huge barrier to the non-member beginner. And they are meant to do so. The business of unions is to protect the membership's

* In Howard Greenberger, *The Off-Broadway Experience* (Englewood Cliffs, NJ: Prentice-Hall, 1971).

ability to land paying jobs, and to keep producers from hiring non-union persons at less than union minimum wages.

You cannot join the unions without a union job, and you cannot get a union job without belonging to the union. This is the big nut you have to crack, and it's a tough one. But there are about 19,000 members in Equity, 30,000 in AFTRA, and another 30,000 members in SAG, so obviously it can be done.*

To get a fair perspective, you must look at the industry from the union's point of view as well as your own. From the outside, your exclusion from many casting opportunities seems unfair; particularly when you find that a producer must pay a fine of $250, in certain jurisdictions and under certain conditions, in order to sign a non-union performer to a union contract. But if you aspire to become a working professional, then you will eventually crack the union, and its regulations will protect *you*. After all, there are thousands of actors coming out of colleges every year who would be only too happy to perform small film roles for $5.00 a day. How can working professionals protect themselves against that? If the union regulations were somehow lifted, chaos would result, and hardly any actor could make a living.

Remember, the union would only get richer (at first) if it accepted initiation fees from everybody who wanted to join. That they do not do this is a testimony that they wish to maintain the integrity of the union as an association of working professionals.

Joining one of the AAAA unions should be a first priority item on your agenda. Only with union membership does the full range of casting and audition opportunities begin to open up to you; most auditions in both New York and Hollywood are posted for Equity actors (or SAG actors) only. Obviously you are going to have to break into one of the off-Broadway, regional theatre, or summer stock shows that will hear non-union auditionees, or one of the television programs or films that screen-tests unknowns. Once you join the union, you can automatically join the others by payment of a fee, which is about half the original initiation fee. Full initiation fees are currently $300 for Equity or SAG (less if you already belong to one of the other AAAA unions), and dues are in the neighborhood of $40 a year.

* These figures cannot be added, of course, because there is considerable duplication.

LIBRARY
EISENHOWER COLLEGE

When you join the union, you can take advantage of union benefits. Each has a regular magazine for members, keeping them up to date on union activities and services. Union offices can offer help and advice, and will act upon complaints about unscrupulous producers or agents. It is important that, during the time you are working toward a position as a professional actor, you keep up your union dues payments and keep in good standing. It is also important that you obey union rules and do not try to act in unauthorized productions that are expressly forbidden by your union.

Your union will provide you with current information about minimum salary scales and working conditions; you should be aware of them and make sure they apply to you. You will be amazed at the number of ways you can be hired and paid according to union-negotiated contracts. The Screen Actors' Guild has negotiated contracts with film producers and television producers that run into hundreds of pages and cover every possible variation of employment. Actors' Equity Association has not only contracted with the League of New York Theatres (the basic contract) and with LORT, but also with COST, CORST, ADTI, MTA, and ACMT, and handles, in addition, an off-Broadway contract, a Hollywood theatre contract, an off-Loop contract for Chicago, a Bay Area contract for San Francisco, a Las Vegas contract, a contract for the producers of industrial shows, a cafe contract, and a guest artist contract. These all differ markedly in their provisions, and you will find that here are hundreds of pay scales for various union dramatic activities.

Ordinarily you will join the union automatically with your first professional job. Ideally, your first salary will cover your initiation cost. If it does not, you will have to have the money available somewhere. A provision of the Taft-Hartley Law will permit you to pay after you have been paid, so that will take some of the sting out of it. In addition, AFTRA rules allow you to do one role, and as many more as you can squeeze into the following 30 days, without joining the union. But 31 days later, your next AFTRA role will require you to join.

How much will you make?

You have a job. Now that you have struggled, humbled yourself, and suffered financial hardships by the carload, you are ready to cash in your chips, right? What will the job pay?

As we've made clear so far, the income of an actor is not great. 1974 SAG figures show a median annual income for all their unionized professionals of *well under* $1000. But if you work you do get paid, and you should know how much that will be.

All the unions have negotiated contracts in your behalf; these contracts specify the minimum salaries you will be paid. The minimum salary scales are written in astonishing detail; the Codified Basic Agreement negotiated between the Screen Actors' Guild and the various motion picture producers is a 172-page book. The contracts are renegotiated continuously upon expiration, so the following information, which is accurate as of this printing, is subject to regular change.

If you landed a part in a Broadway play, your minimum weekly salary would have been $245 in 1974–75, $265 in 1975–76, and $285 in 1976–77. If you went on tour with that show you would make a little over a hundred dollars a week more.

If you landed a part in an off-Broadway play, your weekly salary would have been at least $137.50 in 1974–75, that minimum rises to the Broadway scale as the potential theatre gross reaches $13,000 a week. Off-Broadway theatres reaching for a $10,000 gross, for example, would have paid minimum wages to actors of $158 in 1974–75, $165 in 1975–76, $170 in 1976–77, and $175 in 1977–78.

If you are cast in a resident theatre on the LORT circuit, your salary minimum is determined by the size of the theatre's potential gross just as in the off-Broadway theatres. The "A" Theatres (with potential weekly grosses of $32,000 and up) paid actors $202.45 a week minimum in 1974–75. "B" Theatres ($16,000 gross) paid $176.20, "C" Theatres ($8000 gross) paid $158.70, and "D" Theatres (less than $8000) paid the off-Broadway "minimum minimum" of $137.50. The "A" Theatres, additionally, may employ journeymen, who are signed to special Equity contracts and received, in 1974–75, $125.30 a week. Journeymen contracts "provide training in resident theatres to the advanced student," and are limited in number to 30 percent of the regular equity company members—unless there are more than 30 equity members, in which case there can be any number of journeymen. Dinner theatres and COST and CORST theatres pay roughly the same as LORT theatres. All these union-established minimum salaries are for rehearsal pay as well as actual performance pay.

If you are hired as a paid apprentice, you are not covered by any union contract, so your salary—or stipend—is more or less at the caprice of the management. Fifty dollars a week was a fairly standard non-Equity apprentice stipend in 1974–75.

If you are hired for an outdoor drama, your salary might vary from around $40 to over $200, depending on the show; many of these theatres offer low-cost, company-arranged housing and other incentives as well. Rehearsal salaries are apt to be a bit less, however. To give a single example of this type of operation—*The Lost Colony* (North Carolina) is seen by 75,000 persons a year; it offers 12 weeks of employment, and pays supporting actors $10 to $65 a week ($7.50 to $40 for rehearsals) and principal performers $60 to $90 a week ($40 to $55 for rehearsals), with a total weekly cast payroll of $7233 (1973 figures).

If you find employment in films or television shows, you will be paid either as a day player, a weekly player, or a three-day player (television only). The day player receives $172.50 a day. The three-day player receives $440 for work on a half-hour or hour show, and $517.50 for work on a ninety-minute show. The weekly player draws a minimum of $604. However, on a multiple-week contract for a TV series that minimum drops to $405 (half-hour or hour show) or $477.50 (ninety-minute show). These figures are identical for SAG authorized film work and AFTRA-authorized live (and taped) television work; both unions acted in concert in the 1974 negotiations, and the pact they negotiated runs until 1977.

But these are just scale figures. Obviously you can negotiate (or your agent can negotiate) for more. What are your negotiating tools? They are not the same as those qualities that got you the job in the first place. Your salary will be determined mainly by your name and by the producer's need to have you. An industry is an industry, and nobody is going to spend $1000 for you when he can get someone just as good for $172.50.

Beginners start out at scale, although a featured performer in a television show (more than a couple of lines) will probably get a little more: maybe $200 a day instead of $172.50.

Established performers whose names are known to the industry, if not to the public at large, may get, for a television show, $300 to $400 a day, or perhaps three days work for $900, or a week's work for $1200. Stage actors work for close to minimum figures off-Broadway, and regular actors usually receive from $200 to $400 for stage work on the LORT circuit and for non-starring Broadway roles. While these figures are obviously "rule of thumb," you should realize that a free-lance actor *with a good reputation in the trade* can work fairly regularly and still not make more than $12,000 a year in direct salary payments on television (ten guest spots), films (five weeks' work on each of two films), or live theatre (a 30-week run at $350). That's a living wage, to be sure, but you will have to be very lucky and very good to get it. And next year, of course, you might have half that.

Bigger money comes to the performer who lands a regular run in a television series; this occasionally happens to relatively inexperienced new performers. Even though an unknown performer can start out on a series making as little (relatively) as $405 per week, the regularity of the work multiplies this into a handsome sum. A person contracted to a series is guaranteed at least seven segments and generally will work at least thirteen. Regular salaries of up to $1000 per segment can be paid to virtual newcomers if they are cast as leading series performers, and this mounts steadily as the series goes on year after year. The regulars of *Bonanza* earned $16,000 each per episode in 1971 and negotiated a contract that raised their salary $1000 per segment in succeeding years. Carroll O'Connor, the star of *All in the Family*, reportedly receives a whopping $35,000 per episode. In recent years, however, the number of segments made annually has dropped from 39 to about 15 or 17 for most shows. Established Broadway performers make from $250 to $1000 a week, depending on the size of the part and the size of the budget; the Broadway actor's security comes from the length of an extended run.

With name stars, every rule of thumb goes out the window. A name star is someone whose name alone will bring people to the box office (or bring the Nielsen families to their television sets). Stars, of course, get what the traffic will bear, and several command a million dollars a film. Robert Robert Redford's fee for *Three Days of the Condor* was reported at $1.25 million. Stars may also demand—and get—percentages of the films in which they perform, thereby hitching their salary to the film's success, and reaping giant gains if the film hits. While television and Broadway steer clear of these sums, they still pay well to attract star talent. Rock Hudson received $75,000 for his first *McMillan and Wife* pilot, and guest stars frequently receive upwards of $25,000 for television films. Stars on Broadway receive as much as $25,000 per week, and when you think of the numbers of people they draw into the theatre, you will quickly understand why.

Residuals are an important source of additional income for the television actor. The salary you are paid for acting in a TV production covers its first showing only. For each additional showing you are paid a percentage of your original salary, and the percentage may approach 100 percent—in other words, you may double your original income on a single rerun. The rerun formulas are complex; they escalate from 50 percent to 100 percent in three stages from 1975 to 1977, and are subject to ceilings of $1200 (for ninety-minute shows) $1100 (hour shows) and $1000 (half-hour shows). Summer reruns are only rated at 80 percent residual payment of "in season" ones, and syndicated or non-prime-time reruns are subject to a diminishing scale from 50 percent to 5 percent as the reruns rerun into the dust. Still, it's not at all difficult to imagine that a regularly working television actor will soon be able to expect a tidy continuing income from these sources, particularly since agents' commissions are limited to the first two reruns.

The income potentially available from commercials is, of course, immense, and in 1974 exceeded the earnings of SAG actors in films and on television dramatic fare combined. The performer in a TV commercial is paid a scale wage of $165.90 per shooting day, but then can receive thousands of dollars in residual income as the commercial is flashed across the tube ten times a day for six months. It is not true that the actor collects a residual income for each showing of his commercial—the contracts are extremely complex and confusing in figuring the actual payment—but the average commercial that gets on the air will bring in from $1000 to $3000. A few can net the actor $10,000 or more, and some people—children, housewives, character types—can make upwards of $70,000 to $100,000 annually from this source. A few years ago a nine-year-old girl with no experience walked into an agent's office, was sent on an interview right away, and was hired on the spot to do a toothpaste advertisement. In a single day of toothy grins, nine different commercials were made, and a few years later she was richer by $27,000 for the day's experience.

Still, the working actor must generally be considered in terms of poverty, not riches. Thousands of people try to make a go of it in acting. A few get enough work to keep them going for years—a job here, a job there, a supplement here and there. Of these, only a very few make enough money, in ten years, to go to Sardi's or Chasen's for dinner instead of Howard Johnson's or the Taco Bell. We know that this probably does not interest you now, but will you still enjoy your tacos when you are 45?

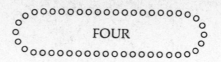
Other opportunities

If you've come this far, where are you? You feel ready to continue a career, and you have a home base, a photo-résumé, an agent, an interview technique, a few good prepared audition scenes, a union card, and a first job. You are at the beginning of a career. Here we leave you. You are now in touch with the sources that can give you the exact personal information and guidance you need. Even at this point, you must remember that there is a 95 percent chance that you will fail at making a livelihood out of acting professionally. Face that fact realistically. In this chapter, we will examine the possibilities of acting professionally outside the established industries of entertainment. You might take a look.

Outside the industry

Everything in this book, so far, is about how an actor accommodates himself to the existing entertainment industries. The theatre, film, and television industries have their own rules and procedures. "You've got to really be *sick* to want to be an actor here" says a well-known Hollywood agent. To be an actor means to stand, sit, smile, and squat on command, and often the command is given by a flagrantly dishonest and unethical old mogul. It means spending most of your life looking for work—even when you are 50—and most of your concentration on where the next job is coming from. It means *schlepping* on your time and at your expense from office to office, from casting director to casting director, and being emotionally and financially subject to a ruling elite in which you may have no personal interest or sympathy.

When you must audition and interview regularly for work (and when that work is both rarely won and transitory), you may begin to develop psychological problems. After all, it is *you* that you are auditioning with, and when rejection is piled atop rejection, something is bound to happen to you. Insecurity nibbles at your psyche. Every job you lose you attribute to a personal flaw. You either may retreat into a shell and self-destruct, or, conversely, stuff yourself with bluster and then fall prey to that. Actors who believe their own bluster become the most pathetic sights in New York and Hollywood; they have become the product they are selling, and as the fine actor Austin Pendleton points out,*

> "Nothing bothers casting people more than the neurotic oversell, and that is because an actor who oversells himself is an actor who does not trust himself and nothing, nothing disturbs show business professionals more than that. Self-mistrust is, after all, the ultimate buried nightmare for anybody in the business, as it is for bullfighters and tightrope-walkers."

Actors are people, and many must fight the contrary desires that war within them: the desire for security versus the lust for fame, the desire for personal happiness versus the need for artistic and emotional freedom. Many actors—even successful ones—find themselves virtual slaves to their profession, and unable to make a personal decision without first consulting their agents, their producers, and their managers. Others enslave themselves to a set of industry conventions that are brutally dehumanizing. The vast majority are poor almost to the point of starvation, and uncounted numbers of them go to jail every year for theft, forgery, and narcotics transactions. In such an unstable atmosphere, homosexuality, pandering, and prostitution flourish. Is this really the world you want to enter? You can see why your parents paled when you told them you wanted to be an actor.

* *Yale Theatre*, Fall 1973.

More and more people, however, are finding acting careers outside of the acting industries today. For those lusting for stardom, these alternatives will not be acceptable, and for countless others they are a compromise.

Educational theatre

The first alternative is what is generally called educational theatre. While America does not have a national theatre, we do have a series of publicly supported theatres in the nation's colleges and universities. These, which began as academic branches of English and speech departments in the 1930's, 40's, and 50's, have become in our time producing organizations that, within obvious limitations, advance live theatre and film art in surprising ways. Numerous professional theatre artists now associate themselves with university theatre establishments, partly for the financial security and prestige that such positions can bring, and partly to have the freedom to work without commercial limitations.

A position with a university drama department will generally require you to teach acting, directing, playwriting, dramatic literature, or theatre technique on a regular basis for the nine-month academic year. You may also be asked to direct plays with students and even to act in them. Depending on the institution, you ordinarily have a high degree of freedom to teach and direct what material you choose. In return for this you are given a reasonable annual salary and, at most institutions, a position with eventual job security (tenure). Drama professors at the top of their profession may earn sizable salaries (over $30,000 at the best institutions) and may be eligible for chairmanships and deanships if they desire to move into administrative areas. There is also the excitement of working with young people and the three months off every year, together with occasional sabbatical leaves with full pay that generally provide another three months off every three years.

Since university theatres are admittedly not wholly professionalized, the position entails more academic credentials than does a Broadway or Hollywood career. Many schools expect their drama faculties to publish books and articles about their specialty—the "publish or perish" formula that has angered so many in the arts and letters faculties of

American colleges. More enlightened universities, however, permit their drama staff to contribute in ways other than publication: by directing plays and acting in them, for example, or by writing plays and filmscripts. This regulation at bottom is a good one; it encourages theatre faculties to strive for a professional level in their various disciplines. The best teachers of acting and directing, one would expect, are those who can move easily between professional and academic engagements, even if they choose not to do so.

Very few people can combine a career in educational theatre with another in the professional world, unless the university that employs them also operates a professional program. Many try for the best of both worlds: the security of teaching and the glamour and riches of Hollywood or Broadway stardom, but very few succeed. To do either well, you must have a massive commitment to it. You can hardly work full time as a university drama professor and audition for Hollywood or Broadway roles between classes. A combination of the two careers, however desirable in theory, is extremely difficult to pull off in practice. One or the other must dominate.

If you are interested in pursuing a career in educational theatre, you must go to graduate school, and beyond that you should do everything in your power to get a doctoral degree: either a DFA or a PhD. Either of these degrees involves a great deal of reading and writing (as well as some acting and directing), and usually the acquisition of one or two foreign languages as well. Do not even think about it if you are not already a dedicated student. Today the MFA degree, which involves less academic work than the doctorate, is also accepted as a valid teaching degree at many smaller colleges and some big ones. As a result, many students prefer to go job hunting at colleges with an MFA in hand, though their prospects frankly are more limited. It is true that many colleges accept non-degreed members for faculty drama positions, but these require enormous proven talent and ability, usually demonstrated by standing as a nationally known artist.

Successful university drama instructors are invariably people who have a love for teaching, for academic freedom, and for the university life. Teaching, on the other hand, may be a very unhappy alternative for the person captivated by the wish to act professionally. A university instructor is not a professional actor or director but a professional educator, and would-be actors who go to graduate school to get a degree "to fall back on" if they fail to make it may never find much satisfaction on a college campus. No matter how professionalized, the academic program is still one of scrutiny and analysis as much as it is of production and performance. It is fascinating to anyone driven by curiosity and a desire for knowledge; it is a supreme bore to anyone looking only for the thrill of the followspot and the fan magazine. It probably involves as much effort to become a successful professor as a successful actor, so it is not recommended that any budding actor "fall back" on the profession of teaching.

Doing your own thing on stage

For the performer who wants to create and perform, but has little or no interest in academia, there is a third alternative between the profession and the campus, and that is the private, non-union theatre company. Some of the most exciting and artistic work in America is currently being done by these companies, current examples of which are the Performance Group in New York, the Teatro Campesino of California, The San Francisco Mime Troupe, the Company Theatre and the proVisional theatre of Los Angeles, The Living Stage in Washington, and various experimental groups gathered around a key figure or leader like Joseph Chaikin, Paul Sills, or Andre Gregory.

These theatres operate outside the established unions or industry. Naturally such groups may have a short life, but some develop an enviable measure of security. Many are communal in both art and living arrangements. Most of these groups perform without salaries and simply try to make ends meet at the box office. Occasionally they are helped out by small grants, and from time to time they establish themselves in a big way and make some money, as Paul Sills's *Story Theatre* group did.

Nothing prevents you from looking up and joining one of these groups, if they will take you, and nothing prevents you from starting up your own. All it takes is a building, some friends, some paint and plywood and some energy and ideas. True, you will have to work in the daytime at "regular" jobs in order to be free to rehearse at night, but if you are doing what makes you happy, you will be well rewarded. For most people the urge to perform need not be satisfied by working on Broadway, in Hollywood, or on the Yale Drama School stage; it could be quite satisfactorily fulfilled by acting with friends before a small audience in your own home town. You should certainly consider this before you pack your bags for either coast. Some of the most genuinely artistic work in the country is done at theatres like these.

As it is true with the theatre, so is it true with the film. The rapid growth of independent, non-studio filmmaking has been one of the outstanding features of the 1960's and early 70's in America; and a large group of non-union amateur filmmakers is growing up nationwide. They have a literature, a character, and an opportunity to exchange presentations. Student and amateur films are being commercially marketed, too, so that a venture into independent filmmaking does not necessarily cut off all professional possibilities.

Even television is opening up into an area of amateur exploitation. Local community antenna television systems (CATV) are initiating local, closed-circuit non-union programming. Coupled with the expected revolution occasioned by cassette broadcasting and the home television systems now appearing on the market, television is no longer going to be under the strict rule of the network executives and sponsors that dominate the industry. Via the nationwide Public Broadcasting System, some of these amateur works may eventually gain a larger audience.

The effect of the contemporary decentralization in theatre, film, and television is to weaken somewhat the position of the entertainment industries. Though the industries still remain fiercely dominant, side routes to performing careers have opened up. The big studios are selling off their back lots and their wardrobes. Broadway and off-Broadway are down in attendance and number of productions, and the LORT circuit and off-off-Broadway are up. Everywhere we see more traces of a grass-roots movement toward artistic expression, unhindered by the industry and reaching for greater exposure.

Undoubtedly the industry will prevail, if only by incorporating, little by little, the changes outside of it. America is a land of corporate amalgamation, and there is no reason to believe that home television will escape the jurisdiction of the unions that will vie for its control—a struggle that is already proceeding. But the artistically dedicated performer must consider this question: Does the industry really serve my purpose, or would I be happier doing what I want to do somewhere else? For more and more people, the latter alternative is getting the nod.

Afterword

This book was dedicated, in its first edition, to 46 acting students who attended the University of California at Irvine between the years 1967 and 1971, and with whom I was more or less personally involved. This was, to a certain extent, a select group, since they had all been cast in plays or programs that I directed, but they were in most other respects typical undergraduates in a University drama program. Only one of them had had professional experience prior to entering UCI, and only one had already taken an undergraduate degree (our graduate program started in the midst of that period). In 1974, I surveyed that group of 46 students to find what they were doing some two to six years following graduation, both in order to evaluate the strength of our program, and to estimate the effectiveness of dramatic instruction in general. Here are the results of that sampling.

Sixteen of the forty-six have received SAG, AGVA, or Equity union cards and are, at this writing, engaged in acting, or in closely related professional fields. Of these, two are regular performers in network series television shows; three have acted in long-running New York shows or national tours; one has appeared in several films and television films; one has become a professional stage manager and producer; one is a concert manager; one has done 15 shows with the Company Theatre

(Los Angeles); one has been with the American Conservatory Theatre; one with the Pittsburg Playhouse; one with the Seattle Repertory Theatre; two with the American Shakespeare Festival Theatre (Connecticut); and two have been involved with Equity productions or SAG films in California. Several of these actors have also made commercials, and several have gone into producing, writing, or directing as well. So far I have been speaking of union employment solely.

Eighteen others have continued to act or have gone into allied fields but have not yet received union cards, or have not found union affiliation necessary at this time. Two are acting with non-union (but paying) companies, three teach drama (college and high school), three are in television and media communications, one is with a New York advertising firm, one is public relations director for an entertainment corporation, three sing in night clubs, one directs plays in Germany, one directs and choreographs children's theatre in Minneapolis, one is a model, one has won a national playwrighting contest and is pursuing that field, one is a production assistant at the Mark Taper Forum (Los Angeles), and three have been making Hollywood rounds with enough success to keep going, but not enough to truly break through.

Of the remaining fourteen, one is the secretary of a professional drama school, three are taking graduate work or advanced conservatory training (Julliard), two have decided to live in a teepee and raise carrots, and seven have proved unreachable. One is a hardware salesman, and considers himself both happy and lucky.

I'm not exactly certain what should be made of these figures, but they are not so dreadfully pessimistic as one might perhaps expect. More than a third of the sample have joined a professional performing union in an average of four years after graduation, and well over two-thirds are clearly en route to professional experience in a theatre or theatre-related field. At least 11 of the sample, representing about 24 percent, have made a reasonable income for at least 2 years running by acting or by producing plays, films, or television shows. These are certainly healthy averages, and probably comparable to the records of recent graduates with BA's in other fields.

So it's not impossible. UC Irvine is, perhaps, a more than usually conducive environment for developing one's professional acting capabilities (the school is performance-oriented, and has a policy of continuously employing professional artists as both guest teachers and resident faculty), and these students, perhaps, were more particularly motivated and dedicated than others; still it is evident that real opportunities for talented, trained, personable, informed, and devoted performers to make significant professional breakthroughs do in fact exist. Whether or not that justifies the search and the hunt and the struggle—that is, of course, a decision that only the actor can make.

Appendix

This is a skeletal book. It is not our intention to provide, in an appendix or elsewhere, a series of addresses that will quickly go out of date, or information that might soon prove factually incorrect. Besides, it will be your job, and you may as well start now, to locate the people you will need to provide you with current factual information on your career. We will, however, help you get started. The following addresses are your first contact points with the industries.

Published information

In New York you can find virtually any material published about acting, including trade papers, journals, and books, at the Drama Book Shop, 150 West 52nd Street (just off Seventh Avenue). You should certainly head there immediately upon arrival in New York. The employees of the Book Shop are usually actors themselves and can offer you good advice. Trade papers are also sold regularly at news stands in the Times Square area.

In Los Angeles you may pick up trade papers around any of the motion picture studios, or at the outdoor magazine stand on Las Palmas near Hollywood Boulevard. Many bookstores line Hollywood Boulevard. One that specializes in your interests is Larry Edmunds' Cinema and Theatre Book Shop, at 6658 Hollywood Boulevard.

Books listing agencies, producers, theatre owners, and the like come out every so often and are available at these outlets. These are *Simon's Directory of Theatrical Materials, Services and Information*, the *Madison Avenue Handbook*, and *Madison Avenue West*. These books contain much information you do not need, but some that you may find valuable, particularly listings of producers of television commercials. Look these books over before you buy, for they are in the $7.00 range.

Books

Books, of course, do not provide you with the most up-to-date information, but here are a few that give good background material on the acting professions:

Joseph Ziegler, *Regional Theatre* (Minneapolis: University of Minnesota Press, 1973). A fine review of the movement and the present condition of LORT.

Theatre Communications Group, *Theatre Profiles* (New York: TCG, 1973). An invaluable listing of nearly 100 nonprofit theatres, with photos of their productions, credos, names, and addresses.

William Goldman, *The Season, A Candid Look At Broadway* (New York: Harcourt Brace & World, 1969). A candid and acid look at the Broadway theatre.

William Bayer, *Breaking Through, Selling Out, Dropping Dead, And Other Notes on Filmmaking* (New York: Delta, 1973). A stunning analysis of Hollywood from a unique point of view.

Uta Hagen, *Respect for Acting* (New York: Macmillan, 1973). A gentle and instructive book on acting written by a fine actress and teacher—particularly interesting because it shows the way a New York actor thinks as well as acts.

Alan Lakein, *How To Get Control of Your Time and Your Life* (New York: McKay, 1973). One young New York actor describes this as *an absolute must.* It may help you achieve a professional attitude.

Lists of franchised agents and producers

Lists of agents are available at the following union offices, but you must pick them up in person.

In New York:

Actors' Equity Association, 1500 Broadway, 10036.

Screen Actors' Guild, 551 West 52nd Street, 10019.

American Federation of Television and Radio Artists, 724 Fifth Avenue, 10019.

In Los Angeles:

Actors' Equity Association, 6430 West Sunset, 90028.

Screen Actors' Guild, 7750 West Sunset, 90046.

American Federation of Television and Radio Artists, 1551 North LaBrea, 90028.

For a start, you can simply find agency listings in the classified sections of the Manhattan and Los Angeles telephone directories, available in your hometown library or telephone company office. Look under "Theatrical Agencies."

Lists of producers are not available from the unions, but you can find most of them in *Simon's Guide* or a similar publication. A less complete (but still valuable) list is found in the yellow pages of the telephone directories of Manhattan and Los Angeles under the heading "Theatrical Managers and Producers." ("Theatrical" in this case applies to all producers—those of television programs, films, and commercials as well as live theatre.) In New York, you can buy the geographical guides to agents and producers, which list them by street as well as alphabetically. These guides, which are published and updated regularly, are available at the Drama Book Shop, and are a must. They are *Agents by Building* ($1.35) and *The Geographical Casting Guide* ($1.75).

Lists of summer theatres

There are about 350 summer theatres in annual operation in this country, and they offer programs that differ enormously. Some are all-Equity - COST, CORST, or MTA companies with stars, and with budgets in the six-figure range. Others are rustic playhouses where the actors live in a barn and build sets between rehearsals (for no pay). The best list of summer theatres, with pertinent information about their programs, apprenticeships, and the like, may be found in *The Summer Theatre Directory*, published annually by the American Theatre Association, Inc. It is available in February from their offices at 1317 F Street, N.W., Suite 500, Washington, DC 20004, or from the Drama Book Shop in New York; the price is $4.00. A similar work, called *Summer Theatre*, is available where trade papers are sold in New York, or from the publisher (*Show Business*) at 136 West 44th Street, New York, NY 10036. Send $3.00.

Lists of regional repertory theatres

The complete list of LORT regional theatres in operation, together with their schedules, is available for 25¢ from the Theatre Communications Group, 355 Lexington Avenue, New York 10017. Some of the oldest of these theatres are listed below.

Actor's Theatre of Louisville
North Seventh Street
Louisville, Kentucky 40202

Alley Theatre
615 Texas Avenue
Houston, Texas 77002

Alliance Theatre Company
1280 Peachtree Street N.E.
Atlanta, Georgia 30309

American Conservatory Theatre
450 Geary Street
San Francisco, California 94102

American Place Theatre
423 West 46th Street
New York, N.Y. 10036

American Shakespeare
  Festival Theatre
1850 Elm Street
Stratford, Connecticut 06497

Arena Stage
Sixth and M Streets S.W.
Washington, D.C. 20024

Asolo State Theatre Company
  (affiliated with URTA)
Postal Drawer E
Sarasota, Florida 33578

Barter Theatre
Main Street
Abingdon, Virginia 24210

Center Stage
11 East North Avenue
Baltimore, Maryland 21202

Center Theatre Group
(Mark Taper Forum)
135 North Grand Avenue
Los Angeles, California 90012

Cleveland Playhouse
2040 East Eighty-sixth Street
Cleveland, Ohio 44106

Goodman Theatre
The Art Institute of Chicago
200 South Columbus Drive
Chicago, Illinois 60603

The Guthrie Theater
725 Vineland Place
Minneapolis, Minnesota 55403

Hartford Stage Company
65 Kinsley Street
Hartford, Connecticut 06103

Indiana Repertory Theatre
411 East Michigan Street
Indianapolis, Indiana 46204

Long Wharf Theatre
222 Sargent Drive
New Haven, Connecticut 06511

Loretto–Hilton Repertory Theatre
130 Edgar Road
St. Louis, Missouri 63119

McCarter Theatre
University Place
Box 526
Princeton, New Jersey 08540

Meadow Brook Theatre
(also plays in Detroit)
Oakland University
Rochester, Michigan 48063

Milwaukee Repertory Theatre
Company
Performing Arts Center
929 North Water Street
Milwaukee, Wisconsin 53202

Negro Ensemble Company
St. Mark's Playhouse
133 Second Avenue
New York, New York 10003

New York Shakespeare Festival
Public Theatre
425 Lafayette Street
New York, New York 10003

The Repertory Theater of
Lincoln Center
Vivian Beaumont Theater
150 West 65th Street
New York, N.Y. 10023

Seattle Repertory Theatre
P. O. Box B
Queen Anne Station
Seattle, Washington 98109

Stage/West
1511 Memorial Avenue
West Springfield, Massachusetts
01089

Studio Arena Theatre
681 Main Street
Buffalo, New York 14203

Trinity Square Repertory Company
87 Weybosset Street, Room 320
Providence, Rhode Island 02903

Virginia Museum Theatre
Boulevard and Grove Avenue
Richmond, Virginia 23220

Washington Theatre Club
1101 23rd Street N.W.
Washington, D.C. 20037

Lists of dinner theatres, outdoor theatres

The American Dinner Theatre Institute, 1341 W. Mockingbird Lane, Suite 233-E, Dallas, Texas 77427 will be able to supply you with a list of their members, although those members constitute only a portion of the dinner theatres actually in existence. *Show Business* magazine (available in New York on the stands, or by a $15 yearly subscription from 136 West 44th Street, New York, NY 10036) frequently gives updated and fuller lists. Outdoor theatres are all listed with the Institute of Outdoor Drama, University of North Carolina, Chapel Hill, North Carolina 27514. A stamped return envelope (and 25¢ for handling; why not?) is always appreciated by these underfunded institutes.

Schools of theatre and acting

Colleges and universities offering major programs in drama are numerous and located everywhere in the country. A complete list is available for $3.00 in the *ATA Directory of American College Theatre*, available at the American Theatre Association, Inc., 1317 F Street N.W., Suite 500, Washington, D.C. 20004. Some colleges are principally graduate schools, while others are primarily undergraduate. Write to those you are interested in, and evaluate their programs and faculties comparatively.

At the risk of excluding some good ones, we offer here a list of several well-respected, permanent noncollegiate schools that offer programs in acting.

In New York:

The American Academy of Dramatic Arts, 120 Madison Avenue, 10016. (Established 1884; offers a two-year course in daytime or evenings to high school graduates).

Herbert Berghof Studio, 120 Bank Street, 10014. (Established 1945; offers courses during four seasonal terms. You may sign up for as few or as many as you wish.)

Sonia Moore Studio of the Theatre, 251 West 80th Street. (Mailing address: 485 Park Avenue, 10022. Offers a program during fall, winter, and spring terms. Admission by interview.)

Neighborhood Playhouse, 340 East 54th Street, 10022. (Offers a full-time program to high school graduates, during which students "are not permitted to seek or accept engagements to appear in public, either on the amateur or professional stage.")

The Lee Strasberg Theatre Institute, 34 West 13th Street, 10011. Offers 12-week courses in acting at various levels.

In Los Angeles:

The Lee Strasberg Theatre Institute, 6757 Hollywood Boulevard, Hollywood, 90028. Offers 12-week courses in acting at various levels.

American Academy of Dramatic Arts/West, 300 East Green Street, Pasadena, 91101.

Inner City Institute for the Performing and Visual Arts. 1308 S. New Hampshire Avenue, Los Angeles, 90006. (Offers degree and extension programs; quite reasonable).

Film Actors Workshop, Burbank Studios, 4000 Warner Boulevard, Burbank, 91505.

Estelle Harmon Actors Workshop, 522 North LaBrea Avenue, Los Angeles, 90036. Offers a wide variety of instruction in stage and video acting.

All of these schools, of course, charge tuition (up to $1400 per year, down to $20 per term, depending on school and courses) and have facilities for study and work. Most present plays before invited audiences of producers and agents.

There are several drama conservatories in the United States, though this is a relatively new development; these are college-level programs that are not degree-oriented, and specialize in theatre instruction to the exclusion of most or all other subjects. Several college campuses have tried, with varying success, to incorporate conservatory-style programs within their undergraduate curricula (New York University, the University of California at Irvine, and the University of Washington, for example). Others begin as conservatories of drama and are not obligated to teach toward a normal BA at all; they usually offer a BFA instead. Among these are

The Juilliard School, Department of Drama, Lincoln Center Plaza, New York, New York 10023.

Goodman School of Drama, 200 South Columbus Drive, Chicago, Illinois 60603.

California Institute of the Arts, 24700 McBean Parkway, Valencia, California 91355.

Where to live and eat in New York and Los Angeles

There are many residences and restaurants in Los Angeles and New York that cater to actors or to young people with little money. The YMCA and YWCA offer rooms for men and women on a daily or weekly basis. The main residential branches of these are:

In New York:

William Sloan House (YMCA), 34th Street and 9th Avenue, 10023 (accepts women too).

East Side YWCA, 138 East 38th Street.

West Side YWCA, 8th Avenue and 51st Street.

In Los Angeles:

Hollywood YMCA, 1553 North Hudson, 90028.

Studio Club (YWCA), 1215 Lodi Place, 90038.

The Y's offer sanitary accommodations, usually with a cafeteria on the premises, for around $20 per week. Women, in addition, can find New York accommodations at The Rehearsal Club, 47 West 63rd Street, New York 10023, which caters exclusively to actresses.

But there are hundreds of cheap hotels and restaurants in both cities. Fairly complete lists may be found in Arthur Frommer's widely available books: *New York on $10.00 a Day* and *Hollywood and Los Angeles on $10.00 a Day*. It is decidedly wise to make reservations (confirmed in writing) in advance of your arrival at any budget hotel.

```
HEIGHT:     5' 10½"                                    VOCAL: Bass
WEIGHT:     150 lbs.                                   EYES & HAIR: Brown

SERVICE (212) JU 6-000   ADDRESS 000 E. 55th St.   HOME CI 7-0000

UNIV. OF PITTSBURGH THEATRE, CHARLES E. MERRILL FELLOWSHIP (M.A. DRAMA), 1973-74
"The Taming of the Shrew"                     Petruchio
"Aria da Capo"                                Thyrsis
"On the Marry-Go-Wrong"                       Topeau
"Mad Dog Blues"                               director
"The Mischievous Machinations of Scapin"      Argante

OFF-BROADWAY, N.Y.C., 1972-73
WORKSHOP FOR THE PLAYERS ART (WPA)            One Act Festival
CLARK CENTER, YWCA                            "The Girls Most Likely to Succeed"
MERCER ARTS CENTER                            "The Two Noble Kinsmen"
ST. CLEMENT'S CHURCH                          "Myth/Oedipus"

AMERICAN SHAKESPEARE THEATRE, STRATFORD, CONN., 1972
"Troilus & Cressida"                          Pandarus
"Antony & Cleopatra"                          Scarus
"Julius Caesar"                               Metellus Cimber, Lucilius (undrstdy)
"Major Barbara"                               Charles Lomax (undrstdy)

REGIONAL THEATRE, 1969-71
UTAH SHAKESPEARE FESTIVAL                      "The Tempest"
                                               "Henry IV, I"
                                               "The Taming of the Shrew"
A.C.T., SAN FRANCISCO                          Training Congress (Scholarship)
                                               "Hadrian VII"
LITTLE THEATRE OF THE ROCKIES, COLORADO        "The Unknown Soldier & His Wife"
                                               "Henry IV, I"

IRVINE REPERTORY COMPANY, UNIV. OF CALIF. AT IRVINE (B.A. DRAMA), 1968-71
"Camino Real"                                 Jacques Casanova
"The Misanthrope"                             Acaste
"The Ticklish Acrobat"                        Mayor Bomogrica
"The Serpent"                                 Player
"Endgame"                                     Hamm
"Rimers of Eldritch"                          Skelly Mannor
"Under Milkwood"                              Captain Cat
"Cabaret"                                     Max

ST. CECILIA'S PLAYERS, QUEENSLAND, AUSTRALIA, 1967
"The Reluctant Debutante"                     David Hoylake-Johnston

FILM
3 shorts, N.Y.U. Grad Film Dept.;  2 full-length, U.C.I. Film Dept.

TRAINING
Curt Conway, Eugene Loring, Brewster Mason, Robert Cohen, U.C.I.
Allen Fletcher, Robert Chapline, Ed Moss, A.C.T.
Elizabeth Smith, AST
Bill Hickey, HB Studio
Herbert Machiz, White Barn Theatre, Westport, Conn.
```

Sample résumé

This is a copy of an actual résumé circulated by an actor.

```
Mr. Boland Wilson
Universal City Studios
100 Universal City Plaza
Universal City, California 91608

Dear Boland:

     You are invited to attend, as my guest, a performance of
The Diary of Anne Frank in which I portray the title role of ANNE
under the supervision of Alex Segal at the University of Southern
California.

     Our show opens Thursday, January 11th and closes Saturday,
January 13th at STOP GAP THEATRE on campus (near Exposition
Boulevard).  Curtain rises at 8:00 p.m.

     I have enclosed a photo and resume along with an addressed
postcard which will reserve a ticket for you and your guest for
the performance of your choice, or you may call 746-SHOW, the USC
box office, and reserve tickets by phone.

     I hope you enjoy our production, and look forward to hearing
your critical comments on my performance.

     Thank you in advance for your interest.

                              Sincerely,

                              (signed)
```

Sample letter

This letter is, according to Boland Wilson, formerly head of talent at Universal Studios, "a perfect example of the kind of invitation that young actors should send to studio and agency personnel." Please note: Do NOT send your letters to Mr. Wilson at this address, because he has moved on to other things as of this writing.

TVQ ratings

These are some sample TVQ ratings, as derived by Marketing Evaluations Inc. and released in 1974 by the Screen Actors' Guild.

Performer	Q Score	Performer	Q Score
Peter Falk	51	Howard K. Smith	22
Jacques Cousteau	41	John Chancellor	21
Charleton Heston	41	Shelley Winters	21
The Carpenters	33	Ernest Borgnine	21
Bette Davis	33	Liza Minelli	17
Kent McCord	31	Beatrice Arthur	17
Richard Boone	29	Diana Ross	16
Greg Morris	29	Ava Gardner	15
Barbara Stanwyk	29	Peggy Lee	13
Agnes Morehead	28	Arthur Godfrey	12
Rod Serling	27	Diahann Carroll	10
Barbara Eden	25	Jack Paar	9
Wilt Chamberlain	25	Jack Cassidy	8
Suzanne Pleshette	24	Jane Fonda	6
Buck Owens	22		

Are some of your favorite actors and actresses on the bottom of the list? Do you wonder why Academy Award winning actress Jane Fonda has one-fourth the TVQ of basketballer Wilt Chamberlain, and one-seventh the Q of underwater explorer Jacques Cousteau? Quite obviously, the image of an unpopular social or political affiliation is a threatening factor in Q ratings.